PREPERS BIBLE

A GUIDE TO PREPARING FOR ALL NATURAL DISASTERS AND SOME PERSONAL TIPS OF SURVIVAL

Why You Should Read This Book

All natural disasters cause loss in some way. Depending on the severity, lives can be lost in any number of disasters. Falling buildings or trees, freezing to death, being washed away, or heat stroke are just some of the deadly effects. Some disasters cause more loss of life than others, and population density affects the death count as well.

This book will show you the best way to prepare for all kinds of natural disaster, including tip and trick for making survival kits, there by providing you the right guardian to prepare/overcome any disaster. Consequently improviing your overall well being...

Table of Contents

INTRODUCTION

The definition of natural disasters is any catastrophic event that is caused by nature or the natural processes of the earth. The severity of a disaster is measured in lives lost, economic loss, and the ability of the population to rebuild. Events that occur in unpopulated areas are not considered disasters. So a flood on an uninhabited island would not count as a disaster, but a flood in a populated area is called a natural disaster.

Examples of Natural Disasters

- Blizzard
- Thunderstorm
- Earth□uake
- Flood
- Hurricane
- Tornado
- Tsunami
- Wildfire

Then there is loss of property, which affects people's living quarters, transportation, livelihood, and means to live. Fields saturated in salt water after tsunamis take years to grow crops again. Homes destroyed by floods, hurricanes, cyclones, landslides and avalanches, a volcanic eruption, or an earth□uake are often beyond repair or take a lot of time to become livable again. Personal effects, memorabilia, vehicles, and documents also take a hit after many natural disasters.

The natural disasters that really affect people worldwide tend to become more intense as the years go on. Frequency of earthquakes, mega storms, and heat waves has gone up considerably in the last few decades. Heavy population in areas that get hit by floods, cyclones, and hurricanes has meant that more lives are lost. In some areas, the population has gotten somewhat prepared for the eventuality of disasters and shelters are built for hurricanes and tornadoes. However, loss of property is still a problem, and predicting many natural disasters isn't easy.

Scientists, geologists, and storm watchers work hard to predict major disasters and avert as much damage as possible. With all the technology available, it's become easier to predict major storms, blizzards, cyclones, and other weather related natural disasters. But there are still natural disasters that come up rather unexpectedly, such as earthquakes, wildfires, landslides, or even volcanic eruptions. Sometimes, a time of warning is there, but it's often very short with catastrophic results. Areas that are not used to disasters affected by flash floods or sudden hail storms can be affected in an extreme way.

Natural disasters occur when natural events occurs and interact with humans. Generally, these natural events become disasters when people have not properly prepared and/or didn't have proper management of the emergency and the result of the natural event is disastrous to those involved.

What is StormAware?

Being StormAware means that you and your family not only know how to protect yourselves in the event of a tornado or severe weather, but that you are aware whenever the weather forecast calls for a chance of severe storms; that during those times you monitor weather for severe weather watches and warnings.

It means that you have planned in advance where you will take shelter at home, work and at other places that you and your family regularly visit.

Being StormAware means you have a NOAA weather radio in case of severe weather warnings in the middle of the night and that you have signed up for severe weather alerts by text message or other means.

Basic Tips

Don't wait for severe weather to arrive to start thinking about keeping yourself and your family safe. Being StormAware means having a plan before severe weather strikes.

EARTHQUAKE

Crawl under a sturdy table and cover your face and head with your arms. Stay away from windows and large bureaus or bookcases that could fall. If you become trapped under debris, cover your mouth with a cloth or shirt, and tap against a pipe or other object to make noise. (Don't yell for help unless you have to; you risk inhaling dangerous ☐uantities of dust.) If you are able, leave the building once the shaking stops--aftershocks can bring down a structure compromised by the initial quake. Finally, if you're outside during the □uake, steer clear of buildings and utility wires.

How to Prepare for Earthquakes

An earth□uake is a natural event that occurs when the tectonic plates in the earth shift, break, and slide together. The resulting release of energy causes the earth to shift and move, and the shaking can cause buildings, bridges, and homes to collapse. In the U.S., earthquakes are most fre□uently associated with the West Coast; however, as many as 45 states across the nation are at risk.

Because earth□uakes are largely unpredictable, make sure your home can withstand intense shaking, no matter where you live. There are several ways you can prepare your home for the threat of an earth□uake. For heavy items that run the risk of toppling, secure them to the wall or floor. This includes strapping water heaters and large appliances to the walls or bolting them to the floor. Any breakable items that could fall should be moved to lower shelves. You should also have your home inspected for cracks in the foundation and any defective wiring or connections, and any repairs should be made as quickly as possible. If you live in an area where earth□uakes are common, consider bolting your home to its foundation.

For family safety, you should understand what to do in the event of an earthquake, such as find shelter beneath a sturdy table or desk. If you've been issued an earthquake warning, to prevent an explosion or fire, the gas and electricity should be turned off. In case of emergency, you should always keep supply of both water and food should as an emergency backup that will last your family for at least three days.

Californians aren't the only ones who need to know earth□uake-safety basics: Forty-five U.S. states and territories are at a moderate or very high risk of earth□uakes, which strike without warning.

How to stay safe: "If you're inside when the shaking starts, drop, cover, and hold on," says Judge. Stay away from windows, protect your head and neck with pillows or blankets, and take cover under a sturdy table or mattress, if possible. If you're outside, find a clear spot—ideally away from buildings, power lines, and trees—drop to the ground, try to cover yourself, and stay put until the shaking stops, says Judge. If you're in a car, find a clear spot, stop, and stay in the car until the □uake is over.

No matter what: Don't run outside. Stay put, and once the quake is over, if you must leave the building, take the stairs instead of an elevator. There could be power outages or aftershocks.

SAFETY TIPS

• Have an earth□uake readiness plan.

• Consult a professional to learn how to make your home sturdier, such as bolting bookcases to wall studs, installing strong latches on cupboards, and strapping the water heater to wall studs.

• Locate a place in each room of the house that you can go to in case of an earth□uake. It should be a spot where nothing is likely to fall on you, like a doorframe.

• Keep a supply of canned food, an up-to-date first aid kit, 3 gallons (11.4 liters) of water per person, dust masks and goggles, and a working battery-operated radio and flashlights in an accessible place.

• Know how to turn off your gas and water mains.

IF SHAKING BEGINS

• Drop down; take cover under a desk or table and hold on.

• Stay indoors until the shaking stops and you're sure it's safe to exit.

• Stay away from bookcases or furniture that can fall on you.

• If you are outdoors, find a clear spot away from buildings, trees, and power lines. Drop to the ground.

• If you are in a car, slow down and drive to a clear place. Stay in the car until the shaking stops.

If you live in a part of the world where earthquakes are common, you probably already know it. That trademark shaking or rolling of the ground is unmistakable. If you're not sure, or want to know if there's any seismic activity in your area, the Global Seismic Hazard Assessment Program and the United States Geological Survey both provide maps that highlight areas of high seismic activity. The USGS also has a live map of seismic activity around the world.

We can tell where in the world it's likely you'll experience an earth□uake, we just can't tell when one will happen and what magnitude it'll be when it does. Because of this, preparation is critical. What you do in and after an earth□uake may save your life, but what you do beforehand almost certainly will.

There's nothing you can do to actually avoid the effects of an earthquake. All you can really do is make sure you understand the difference between a minor one and a serious one, and prepare accordingly.

Make sure you have a disaster plan. As with our other disasters, a disaster plan for an earth□uake is important. However, because earth□uakes can strike suddenly and without warning, and in some cases they can lead to other problems like fires or tsunamis, it's critical to have a disaster plan for your household and family, and to have practiced it so it's second nature when you need to act on it.

Give your home an earth□uake checkup. Check for hazards, fasten shelves to wall studs, and store breakables and poisons in cabinets that latch shut so they won't fall out and onto someone in an earthquake. Put heavy objects on lower shelves, and secure heavy furniture, either by fastening it to the wall or blocking rollers so they won't slide around. Make any structural repairs to the walls or foundation that are necessary.

Practice drills with your family (or coworkers.) Know where the utility shut-off switches are in the house, and time yourself getting from your bedroom out of the house to a safe location. Time yourself doing the same again, but shutting off utilities and grabbing your go bag, documents, and checking on family members along the way. In a real emergency, you may not have time for any of that, but it's important to see if it's possible.

Familiarize yourself with common earthquake myths. Earth□uake myths abound, and many keep people from doing the safe thing in an emergency. For example, you may have heard that in an earthquake you should stand in a doorframe to protect yourself from collapsing walls. That's not true at all: Doorframes in most homes are lightly constructed and will collapse easily. Ready.gov notes you should only stand in a doorway if you know for fact that it's sturdy and load-bearing in your home. Other myths, like "earthquakes only happen in the morning," and "hot and dry equals earthquake weather," are all similarly false. The idea you should shelter next to furniture instead of under it is also untrue. Finally, don't assume that earthquakes are a California, west coast thing. Nothing could be further from the truth.

TORNADO

Once you hear a storm warning, tune to a NOAA weather radio for tornado alerts. If an alert comes, seek refuge in a basement--either your own or a neighbor's--or go to an emergency shelter. As a last resort, stay on the lowest floor of your home. If you're in a car as a tornado approaches, get out and seek shelter indoors. If you're caught in the open, lie flat in a ditch or depression and cover your head with your hands.

How to Prepare for Tornadoes

A tornado involves winds that can travel as fast as 250 to 300 miles per hour. These winds can destroy buildings, and turn objects, including cars, into projectiles that can harm people and property. You can take steps to protect your home from a tornado, but if your home is in the direct path of a tornado it may not be possible to completely prevent damage.

Especially if you live in an area prone to tornadoes, make sure to take steps to help secure your home. As with hurricanes, shutters may be added to protect windows from shattering. Garages should be fortified and some people may choose to have a safe room installed for the safety of their families. You should also schedule a home inspection and have the house and roof checked, and make any repairs as necessary.

If a tornado becomes a threat, have a place where you can go. Some homeowners prefer to have a safe room installed, but a basement is also a good choice in case of a tornado. If the home has neither a basement nor safe room, then the ideal place to seek shelter is the center of the home, away from windows or outer walls. If outdoors, a person should seek shelter or lay flat in an open field. People should not stay in a car or under a bridge or overpass as these areas are unsafe. If a tornado approaches, seek cover and do not stay outside or attempt to outrun a tornado.

Tornados, violent rotating columns of air that can uproot trees and peel off roofs, have been reported in every state, but they are more common in the midwestern plains states.

How to stay safe: If you hear tornado sirens or a tornado warning has been issued for your area, it means a tornado has been detected and there's immediate danger. Take shelter immediately in a basement or a small interior room away from windows—a closet, a bathroom, a hallway. Get under a sturdy table or a mattress if you can. "If you're in bed, pull pillows or a bedspread—anything—over the top of you," says Judge.

If you're in a car, get to a sturdy building if possible. If this is not possible, you have two options. One is stay in the car, buckle the seat belt, cover your head with your hands or a blanket, and duck below the windows. The second option, if there is a ditch nearby, is to get out of the car and lie down in the ditch and cover your head. You'll have to base your decision on your particular circumstances.

No matter what: Don't get on an elevator. You could be trapped if the power goes out. If you're on a high floor, take the stairs.

Don't assume that because you may not live in an area that's specifically prone to tornadoes that you're not at risk. Anywhere a thunderstorm can appear, a tornado can too. The amount of concentrated damage they can inflict is stunning. As with most storms, the best way to handle a tornado is to get out of its way and steer clear.

There's little you can do to actually "prepare" a home or business for a tornado. Their destructive power is simply too immense for you to just armor up and go on about your business. Here's what you can do, however:

Make sure you have a disaster plan. We may sound like a broken record now, but it's still important. If a tornado warning is issued for your area, you and everyone in your household or office should know what to do and where to take shelter.

Familiarize yourself with the warning signs. Tornadoes are usually accompanied by other strong storms, like thunderstorms or hurricanes, but not always. Watch the sky— the sky will get dark suddenly, and you may hear a loud rushing sound, almost a roar. The wind may pick up for a while, but suddenly die down. Watch for clouds beginning to rotate in a circular pattern. Tornadoes may strike quickly—the trademark funnel cloud is a good sign, but the cloud doesn't take on that tone until the cloud descends or debris is picked up. They may be transparent before that.

Learn the truth about tornado myths. "Tornadoes don't cross rivers or bodies of water." "Tornadoes don't happen in the mountains or on rough terrain." Both of these are false (The Great Natchez Tornado of 1840 moved along the Mississippi river for miles, and just few years bach a tornado in the Colorado mountains was the 2nd highest on record), and there are more where those came from. Don't get caught following superstition or old wives' tales in the middle of a life-threatening emergency.

Listen to emergency radio. We've said this before too, but it's just as important. Severe weather information is often first communicated by NOAA Weather Radio. Secondhand reports like weather apps, television news, or talk/music radio may also convey useful information, but they'll always be moments behind. Listen for emergency broadcasts if the conditions look right for a tornado, or if you're in the middle of a severe thunderstorm.

Understand the difference between a tornado watch and a tornado warning. A tornado watch means the conditions are right for a tornado to develop. A tornado warning means one has been sighted and you should seek shelter immediately.

Quick Tornado Facts

- Parents should make sure their children know:
- What a tornado is
- What tornado watches and warnings are
- What county or parish they live in (warnings are issued by county or parish)

- How to take shelter, whether at home or at school

Create a plan for where you and your family will go in the event of a tornado — at home, at work and at relatives' or friends' homes that you visit fre☐uently. Always be alert to changing weather conditions.

Pick a safe room in your home where household members and pets may gather during a tornado. This should be a basement, storm cellar or an interior room on the lowest floor with no windows.

Check with your work and your children's school and day care center regarding tornado emergency plans. Every building has different safe places. It is important to know where they are and how to get there in an emergency.

Make sure everyone understands how tornado siren warning systems work and if a warning system is installed in your area.

Mark clearly where your first-aid kit and fire extinguishers are located. Make sure the first-aid kit is properly stocked with medical supplies.

Teach your family how to administer basic first aid, how to use a fire extinguisher, and how and when to turn off water, gas, and electricity in your home.

Mark clearly where the utility switches or valves are located so they can be turned off – if time permits – in an emergency.

FLOOD

If a flash-flood warning is issued, move to higher ground immediately--don't wait to gather belongings. In any flood, avoid downed powerlines and moving water. Six inches of moving water can make a pedestrian fall, while a foot will float most vehicles.

How to Prepare for Flooding

Prepare for Flooding

Flooding is a natural disaster that can affect anyone, regardless of where they live. In the U.S. it is in fact the most common type of natural disaster, with flash-floods causing an estimated 200 deaths annually. To protect yourself in the event of a flood, you should always seek higher ground. Don't attempt to drive—driving through flood waters could cause your vehicle to become stuck and even swept away.

There are steps you can take to protect your property before a flood occurs. One way to protect your property from water damage is to seal the basement walls with waterproof compounds. If possible, flood walls may also be constructed to help stop the possible flow of floodwaters before it reaches your home. You should also have a sump pump, as well as a backup that operates on batteries. Electrical components and the water heater, washer and dryer, and furnace should be elevated no less than 12 inches above any assumed flood levels. If constructing a new home in an area that is located in a flood zone, it should be elevated and reinforced.

Taking some steps to protect your home ahead of time will help curtail any costly damage due to flooding.

Flash floods occur suddenly and due to quickly rising waters caused by heavy rains over a short time period. Aside from making everything soggy, they can be powerful enough to uproot trees and sweep away bridges.

How to stay safe: Monitor local media during heavy rains. In the event of a flash-flood watch, "you want to be prepared to evacuate at a moment's notice," says Judge. A flash-flood warning means flooding is happening or will soon occur in your area and you should seek higher ground immediately.

No matter what: Don't drive or walk through rising water. "Most cars can be swept away by less than two feet of moving water," says Judge. In fact, a high percentage of flood deaths happen in vehicles. Instead, turn around and drive to higher ground, or leave the car and run to higher ground if the road is blocked.

Floods and tsunami can happen on regular schedules or they can be complete surprises. Tsunami are series of large waves triggered by undersea earthquakes or major disruptions on the sea floor. The amount of time you have to prepare or get to higher ground depends entirely on how close to the shore the disturbance was. Flooding is a little more predictable, but not necessarily. Flash flooding can occur in areas where there's been no rain. There's a great deal of data on regional flood plains and areas with histories of flooding, but don't assume that because you don't live in said region, it can't happen to you. With planning and research beforehand though, neither have to take you by surprise. Photo by Thomas Good.

With floods and tsunami, preparation is absolutely key. Flooding can go from a trickle to multiple feet in no time, and in the case of tsunami, storm surges can wash away entire buildings in minutes. Dr. Bradley notes that these disasters, tsunami specifically, are subject to his Cardinal Rule: That some disasters can only be survived by getting out of their way. Here's how to prepare:

Make sure you have a disaster plan. Specific gear won't generally help you in a flood or a tsunami's surge, but things like food and fresh water, medication, water purification tablets, and a first aid kit definitely will. What's more important in this case though is that you have a plan that you and others can put into motion quickly to get out of a dangerous area and to higher ground. It's essential to practice your escape plan with family members so you can get to a meet-up point quickly and safely.

Visit the Federal Emergency Management Agency's flood map database. Use the tool to see if you live in a flood plain or area at high risk for flooding, and how often that flooding normally occurs. You can also use topographical maps to find out where the highest points in your community or area are, so you can head there if a flood or tsunami occurs. If you're a property owner, get flood insurance from the National Flood Insurance Program.

Make sure you have an emergency radio. Tsunami warnings are usually issued by NOAA's Tsunami Warning Center, and it's important to tune in after an earthquake to find out whether a tsunami warning has been issued. Flood and flash flood warnings are also issued by NOAA, so make sure you have a radio that can tune in to NOAA Weather Radio.

During a flood or a tsunami, the critically important thing is to get out of the water and to higher ground. Tsunami are generally violent, fast, and destructive—much more so than they may appear at first glance. What looks like a slow-moving cascade of water from above is actually a rushing wave dozens of feet high to someone caught in it. If you don't believe me, the video here was taken with a dashboard camera during the 2011 tsunami in Japan. It goes from happily driving to a bobbing bubble of metal floating in the water in less than four minutes. Here's what to do if you're caught in a sudden flood or rush of water:

Listen to emergency radio. There's no way for you to tell whether what you're experiencing is a flood, a flash flood, or how high the waters will get. If an evacuation order is given, you'll need to pay attention to emergency services to hear it. Listening to emergency radio can make the difference between moving to a higher floor in your home or apartment building and needing to leave your home entirely for safer ground.

If you're driving, do not pass through standing water, or water where you cannot see the bottom. Six inches of water will reach the bottom of most cars, causing control issues. If that water gets into the engine, your car will stall. Six inches is all it takes. A foot is enough to float a car or truck. Two feet will carry almost any vehicle off, including SUVs. Don't be deceived by what looks like a little water either—the road underneath may have washed away, making it deeper than it appears, especially at night. Don't risk your vehicle or your life. Pull over, drive around, or get out and get to higher ground.

If you're walking, do not walk through moving or rushing water. A few inches can make you fall down, and fast-moving water can carry a person off ⬚uickly. If you have to walk through water, look for where the water isn't moving. Stay away from streams, sewer drains, and manmade channels or drainage canals.

If there is any possibility of a flash flood, or you think a tsunami is imminent get to higher ground immediately. Don't wait for instructions or an official warning—just get your go-bag, important documents, family members, and go as soon as possible. "Trust your instincts and take action," Dr. Bradley explains. If an actual flood warning has been issued, do the same and evacuate for higher ground immediately. Make sure you know the difference between a warning and a watch.

If you time to evacuate your home, turn off utilities and move critical items to the highest possible point. Do this only if you have time, but if you live in a floodplain, you may have some warning. Make sure you know where gas, water, and power cut-off valves are, and disconnect any appliances you can. Of course, don't touch any wires, plugs, or other electrical e☐uipment if you're standing in water

Many of the rules post-flood are the same as during a flood. Just because the water starts to recede doesn't mean it's gone where you want to go. Don't walk into moving or deep water just because the storm has passed or rushing water has receded. Keep your ears on emergency radio, and stay out of the way of emergency service personnel who may be working to help people who have been trapped by the waters.

Keep in mind that any flooded area is prone to additional flooding if conditions pick back up. Even a little rain can turn a once flooded area into a sudden flash flood. Also, floodwaters may have swept debris and other hazardous materials into an area. Look out for glass, downed power lines, ruptured gas lines, damaged buildings, and so on. Floodwater itself can be contaminated by gasoline, oil, sewage, or other chemicals—another reason to stay out of any of it, even if it's standing water. Do not return to a flooded area until authorities indicate that it's safe.

HURRICANE

Heed evacuation orders, first shutting off utilities ("Shut Down Your Home in 5 Minutes"). If you stay home, turn off gaslines and fill your tub with water. Secure shutters. During the storm, move to an interior room and close all doors.

How to Prepare for Hurricanes

Lives and property are lost on a yearly basis as a result of hurricanes. These low pressure tropical storms are common in the Gulf Coast, and can cause damage to property as a result of wind or flooding. If you live in an area with hurricanes, it's important to fortify your home against a hurricane before one occurs.

To protect yourself from the damages caused by hurricanes, you should have garage doors fortified, and add clips or straps to your roof to help maintain its structure. Add some permanent storm shutters to help protect windows from damage. You may also consider building a safe room in your home or basement. These are rooms that are designed to withstand extreme winds and resulting projectiles. Proper insurance is also important for people who live in areas known for hurricanes. Because hurricanes are often accompanied by tornadoes and flooding from heavy rainfall, a home should have adequate flood and wind coverage (see our section on floods).

Learn your community's evacuation plan in case of a hurricane, and do not attempt to wait it out if you're issued an evacuation warning.

June through November is hurricane season in the Atlantic Ocean, the Caribbean Sea, and the Gulf of Mexico, where storms with unassuming names like Wilma and Andrew can be catastrophic. Fortunately, meteorologists can forecast storms days before they make landfall, so you should have time to make an emergency plan or evacuate.

When the storm hits: "You want to get away from windows that might blow in," says James Judge, the executive director of Lake Emergency Medical Services, in Mount Dora, Florida, and a member of the American Red Cross Scientific Advisory Council. If you have a basement, shelter there. If not, choose an interior room on the lowest floor with no windows, like a bathroom or a closet, and take essential supplies—water, food, radio, batteries, flashlight—with you. Lie on the floor under a sturdy object, like a table, or cover yourself with blankets and pillows. If you're in a car or outdoors when the storm hits, seek refuge in the nearest building. If you think the storm is over, check reports on the radio. You might be in the hurricane's calm eye and winds will soon return.

No matter what: Don't try to evacuate once the storm has reached you. "If the wind is blowing and the rain is coming down, you've waited too long,"

Generally we see hurricanes coming from miles away, and we have the technology to forecast how severe a hurricane will be when it gets close enough to us to matter. This is a double-edged sword though; what you do beforehand matters, but because the real threat won't show up for hours or days, it's easy to ignore. Hurricanes are still dangerous and deadly, and shouldn't be underestimated. Here's what to do. Photo by NASA Goddard Space Flight Center.

Preparation is critical if you're in the path of a hurricane, or if you live in an area where hurricanes are freuent. Remember, hurricanes can be dangerous enough, but they can bring flooding, thunderstorms, and tornadoes with them, along with sustained rains and winds, so you should think as though you're preparing for those disasters as well.

Make sure you have a disaster plan. Your disaster plan, go bag, and important documents are more important here than in many other cases. You'll likely have enough warning to get them and evacuate if an order is issued, but you probably won't have time to assemble them if the storm is coming. Do yourself a favor and do it beforehand, and Make sure your family understands what to do if the storm arrives and you're not all in the same place together. A 72 hour kit with food and water is especially important for a slow-moving storm like a hurricane, which can knock out power for days and cut off potable water supplies. Make sure you have water, either by buying it or filling bathtubs and toilets with fresh water before the storm hits.

Prepare your home. If you're a homeowner (or you live in an area prone to hurricanes), you can board up your windows with plywood or install storm shutters, secure your roof and siding to your house frame with straps. Reinforce garage doors, trim back long branches, bring in outdoor furniture, and so on. Check the Federal Emergency Management Agency's flood map database to determine if your home is in an area prone to flooding. Check where the highest ground in your area is, just in case.

Familiarize yourself and your family with utility shut-off switches and valves in your home in case you have to evacuate.

Familiarize yourself with emergency evacuation routes and shelters. If an evacuation order is issued, you don't want to wonder which path is the best and safest out of town. Check with your local emergency management agency to see what the designated evacuation routes in each direction are, and commit them to memory (or draw them out on a paper map and stash it in your vehicle.) Also make sure you're aware of any community shelters in your neighborhood, or buildings that qualify as shelters (like old fallout shelters with deep basements, for example.)

Prepare for travel. If an evacuation order is issued, you want to make sure your vehicle is ready to leave, or you have a way to get out of town safely. Make sure your car's gas tank is full, important items are already stowed in the car, and any repairs that might impede your evacuation are done. Make sure there's a first aid kit in your car (as well as in your go-bag and with your disaster kit.)

Even weaker hurricanes are still hurricanes, and can cause serious damage. If you haven't been told to evacuate, you're likely safe sheltering in place, but you should still be alert and aware of what's going on outside. The order to evacuate can come quickly, even if everything else seems like it's going well. Remember, in many cases it's not the hurricane itself that does the damage, but the storm surge—or water that's pushed ashore by the hurricane's fierce winds and motion. Much of the damage from Hurricane Sandy, for example, was caused by the surge, not the winds and rain.

Monitor emergency radio, news radio, or television news for relevant information. Paying attention to emergency radio can keep you up to date on whether an evacuation order has been issued for your area, but local news in this case can keep you up to date on how your neighbors are faring and when it'll be safe to go out to other parts of town.

Secure your home and shelter in place. Now is the time to put into motion all of the preparation you did before the storm struck. If you didn't need to reinforce your home, close the blinds, move important items away from the windows, and secure them. Stay away from the windows yourself. Close interior doors, and stay as far to the interior of your home as possible.

Obey evacuation orders. If an order is issued for your area, leave immediately. Grab your go bag, disaster kit, any important documents and items, and leave as uickly as possible along evacuation routes. Don't try to pack your car after the order is issued—grab what you can and go.

Don't be fooled if there's a lull in the storm or if conditions seem to suddenly improve. You may be experiencing the eye of the storm, and the winds and rain will return soon. It may be a good time to evacuate or get to a shelter if you've been instructed to, but don't think the storm is over.

Hurricanes can often leave the type of destruction in their wake that resemble floods, thunderstorms, and tornadoes all in one. If you've sheltered in place, odds are it'll be safe to leave once the hurricane has passed over, although you may still see thunderstorms in your forecast. Continue to monitor local weather conditions and emergency radio before you head out.

If you're without power, avoid using candles (for fire safety reasons) and try to use flashlights to get around.

If you were evacuated, check with authorities that it's safe to return before going back. Remember, there may be flooding or standing flood water, so just because the storm has passed, it may not be safe to return. There may not be power, there may be ruptured gas lines in the area, contaminated water, or damaged structures in the wake of a damaging hurricane. When you are able to return, inspect your home and take note of any damage. Report it as soon as possible to the appropriate authorities. Throw out any spoiled food that may have been in your fridge or freezer while you were without power, and stay alert for additional trailing storms or wind that may follow the hurricane.

How to Prepare for Wildfires

Like many natural disasters, wildfires can happen anywhere. Once started, a wildfire will often spread fast, destroying vegetation, wildlife, and property in its path. Most often they start in forests, remote hills, mountain areas, or other woodland settings. Take note that areas with drought are especially susceptible to wildfire. Wildfires are often triggered by natural occurrences such as lightning; however, human carelessness can also cause wildfires.

If you live in an area especially vulnerable to wildfire, there are steps you can take to secure your home. When you build a home, you'll want to avoid using any type of combustible material on your roof, or on any other part of the home. When using wood to construct any part of the home, it should be fire-resistant treated wood. Or opt for fire-resistant materials, such as stucco or fiber cement.

You can also take steps around your home's perimeter to help prevent wildfire damage. Around the outside of the house, shrubs and other plants should be of a fire-resistant variety and should help contain as opposed to fuel fire. Lawn furnishings and any items that could easily burn should be moved away from the home so that it is outside of what is considered the defensible space. You should also have a hose that is long enough to reach around the entire house.

If warned of an approaching fire, keep all windows and doors shut, turn off the gas, wet the roof, and evacuate as instructed.

Wildfires, which happen most often in the west, burn several million acres of U.S. woodland every year.

How to stay safe: "In a wildfire, truly every second counts,"They spread □uickly, igniting trees and homes." If a wildfire is burning in your area, monitor the fire reports on local media and be prepared to evacuate at a moment's notice. Close windows and doors to minimize smoke exposure, and stay away from outside walls. If you're in a car and a fire is approaching, roll up the windows, close the vents, and drive slowly. If there's no escape route and you have to stop, stay in the car, get on the floor, and cover up with a blanket or a coat.

No matter what: Don't try to stand your ground with a garden hose. "You don't stand a chance. "Save yourself and your family. You can always replace your possessions."

How to Prepare for Hailstorms

Hail is frozen drops of rain that circulate in a thunderstorm until they become too heavy and fall. When these chunks of ice fall, the force can dent vehicles or even crash through roofs. Hail often falls in storms where large amounts of hail fall at one time, often accompanying thunderstorms.

There is little that you can do to prepare your home for hail. In areas where hailstorms are fre□uent, you may consider replacing an old roof with an impact-resistant one. Likewise, because hail can shatter windows, it's a good idea to install double-pane windows, and keep your shades or blinds drawn during a hailstorm. To protect yourself, it is important to move indoors and away from windows when a hailstorm begins.

How to Prepare for Volcanic Eruptions

Prepare for Volcanic Eruptions

When a volcano erupts it spews molten lava and ash that will devastate anything that it comes in contact with. In the event of a volcanic eruption there is nothing that can be done to save a home that is in the path of lava. In this case, you should consider your safety and evacuate the home.

If not in the direct path of lava flow, you may not be advised to evacuate. Keep your windows and doors closed to minimize the amount of ash that enters your home. Place moistened towels in front of closed doors and windows to prevent lava or ash from entering on a draft. If lava threatens your home, you should also cover and unplug all electronics. You should also

keep emergency food and water for your family for three days,
in case it's needed.

The 20 safest countries, according to the report

Qatar - 0.1%

Malta - 0.61%

Barbados - 1.16%

Saudi Arabia - 1.32%

Grenada - 1.44%

Iceland - 1.55%

Kiribati - 1.78%

Bahrain - 1.81%

United Arab Emirates - 2.1%

Sweden - 2.26%

Finland - 2.28%

Egypt - 2.34%

Norway - 3.35%

Israel - 2.49%

Singapore - 2.49%

Estonia - 2.52%

Seychelles - 2.58%

Switzerland - 2.61%

Luxembourg - 2.68%

Oman - 2.74%

The 20 least safe

Vanuatu - 36.43%

Tonga - 28.23%

Philippines - 27.52%

Guatemala - 20.88%

Bangladesh - 19.81%

Solomon Islands - 18.11%

Costa Rica - 16.94%

Cambodia - 16.9%

El Salvador - 16.85%

Timor-Leste - 16.37%

Papua New Guinea - 15.9%

Brunei Darussalam - 15.58%

Mauritius - 15.18%

Nicaragua - 14.89%

Japan - 14.1%

Fiji - 13.56%

Guinea-Bissau - 13.09%

Vietnam - 12.81%

Chile - 12.28%

Jamaica - 12.15%

Earthquakes are a common occurrence, rumbling below Earth's surface thousands of times every day. But major earthquakes are less common. Here are some things to do to prepare for an earthquake and what to do once the ground starts shaking

Maslow's (1943, 1954) hierarchy of needs is a motivational theory in psychology comprising a five tier model of human needs, often depicted as hierarchical levels within a pyramid.

Maslow stated that people are motivated to achieve certain needs and that some needs take precedence over others. Our most basic need is for physical survival, and this will be the first thing that motivates our behaviour. Once that level is fulfilled the next level up is what motivates us, and so on.

maslow's hierarchy of needs five stage pyramide

This five stage model can be divided into deficiency needs and growth needs. The first four levels are often referred to as deficiency needs (D-needs), and the top level is known as growth or being needs (B-needs).

The deficiency needs are said to motivate people when they are unmet. Also, the need to fulfil such needs will become stronger the longer the duration they are denied. For example, the longer a person goes without food, the more hungry they will become.

One must satisfy lower level deficit needs before progressing on to meet higher level growth needs. When a deficit need has been satisfied it will go away, and our activities become habitually directed towards meeting the next set of needs that we have yet to satisfy. These then become our salient needs. However, growth needs continue to be felt and may even become stronger once they have been engaged. Once these growth needs have been reasonably satisfied, one may be able to reach the highest level called self-actualization.

Every person is capable and has the desire to move up the hierarchy toward a level of self-actualization. Unfortunately, progress is often disrupted by a failure to meet lower level needs. Life experiences, including divorce and loss of a job may cause an individual to fluctuate between levels of the hierarchy. Therefore, not everyone will move through the hierarchy in a uni-directional manner but may move back and forth between the different types of needs.

Maslow noted only one in a hundred people become fully self-actualized because our society rewards motivation primarily based on esteem, love and other social needs.

The original hierarchy of needs five-stage model includes:

1. Biological and Physiological needs - air, food, drink, shelter, warmth, sex, sleep.

2. Safety needs - protection from elements, security, order, law, stability, freedom from fear.

3. Love and belongingness needs - friendship, intimacy, trust and acceptance, receiving and giving affection and love. Affiliating, being part of a group (family, friends, work).

4. Esteem needs - achievement, mastery, independence, status, dominance, prestige, self-respect, respect from others.

5. Self-Actualization needs - realizing personal potential, self-fulfillment, seeking personal growth and peak experiences.

Maslow posited that human needs are arranged in a hierarchy:

"It is quite true that man lives by bread alone — when there is no bread. But what happens to man's desires when there is plenty of bread and when his belly is chronically filled?

At once other (and "higher") needs emerge and these, rather than physiological hungers, dominate the organism. And when these in turn are satisfied, again new (and still "higher") needs emerge and so on. This is what we mean by saying that the basic human needs are organized into a hierarchy of relative prepotency" (Maslow, 1943, p. 375).

The expanded hierarchy of needs:

It is important to note that Maslow's (1943, 1954) five stage model has been expanded to include cognitive and aesthetic needs (Maslow, 1970a) and later transcendence needs (Maslow, 1970b).

Changes to the original five-stage model are highlighted and include a seven-stage model and a eight-stage model, both developed during the 1960's and 1970s.

1. Biological and Physiological needs - air, food, drink, shelter, warmth, sex, sleep, etc.

2. Safety needs - protection from elements, security, order, law, stability, etc.

3. Love and belongingness needs - friendship, intimacy, trust and acceptance, receiving and giving affection and love. Affiliating, being part of a group (family, friends, work).

4. Esteem needs - self-esteem, achievement, mastery, independence, status, dominance, prestige, managerial responsibility, etc.

5. Cognitive needs - knowledge and understanding, curiosity, exploration, need for meaning and predictability.

6. Aesthetic needs - appreciation and search for beauty, balance, form, etc.

7. Self-Actualization needs - realizing personal potential, self-fulfillment, seeking personal growth and peak experiences.

8. Transcendence needs - helping others to achieve self actualization.

maslow's hierarchy of needs five stage pyramide

Self-actualization

Instead of focusing on psychopathology and what goes wrong with people, Maslow (1943) formulated a more positive account of human behavior which focused on what goes right. He was interested in human potential, and how we fulfill that potential.

Psychologist Abraham Maslow (1943, 1954) stated that human motivation is based on people seeking fulfillment and change through personal growth. Self-actualized people are those who were fulfilled and doing all they were capable of.

The growth of self-actualization (Maslow, 1962) refers to the need for personal growth and discovery that is present throughout a person's life. For Maslow, a person is always 'becoming' and never remains static in these terms. In self-actualization a person comes to find a meaning to life that is important to them.

As each individual is unique the motivation for self-actualization leads people in different directions (Kenrick et al., 2010). For some people self-actualization can be achieved through creating works of art or literature, for others through sport, in the classroom, or within a corporate setting.

Maslow (1962) believed self-actualization could be measured through the concept of peak experiences. This occurs when a person experiences the world totally for what it is, and there are feelings of euphoria, joy and wonder.

It is important to note that self-actualization is a continual process of becoming rather than a perfect state one reaches of a 'happy ever after' (Hoffman, 1988).

Maslow offers the following description of self-actualization:

'It refers to the person's desire for self-fulfillment, namely, to the tendency for him to become actualized in what he is potentially.

The specific form that these needs will take will of course vary greatly from person to person. In one individual it may take the form of the desire to be an ideal mother, in another it may be expressed athletically, and in still another it may be expressed in painting pictures or in inventions' (Maslow, 1943, p. 382–383).

Are you self-actualized?

Characteristics of self-actualized people

Although we are all, theoretically, capable of self-actualizing, most of us will not do so, or only to a limited degree. Maslow (1970) estimated that only two percent of people would reach the state of self-actualization. He was especially interested in the characteristics of people whom he considered to have achieved their potential as individuals.

By studying 18 people he considered to be self-actualized (including Abraham Lincoln and Albert Einstein) Maslow (1970) identified 15 characteristics of a self-actualized person.

Characteristics of self-actualizers:

- They perceive reality efficiently and can tolerate uncertainty;
- Accept themselves and others for what they are;
- Spontaneous in thought and action;
- Problem-centered (not self-centered);
- Unusual sense of humor;

- Able to look at life objectively;
- Highly creative;
- Resistant to enculturation, but not purposely unconventional;
- Concerned for the welfare of humanity;
- Capable of deep appreciation of basic life-experience;
- Establish deep satisfying interpersonal relationships with a few people;
- Peak experiences;
- Need for privacy;
- Democratic attitudes;
- Strong moral/ethical standards.

Behavior leading to self-actualization:

(a) Experiencing life like a child, with full absorption and concentration;

(b) Trying new things instead of sticking to safe paths;

(c) Listening to your own feelings in evaluating experiences instead of the voice of tradition, authority or the majority;

(d) Avoiding pretense ('game playing') and being honest;

(e) Being prepared to be unpopular if your views do not coincide with those of the majority;

(f) Taking responsibility and working hard;

(g) Trying to identify your defenses and having the courage to give them up.

The characteristics of self-actualizers and the behaviors leading to self-actualization are shown in the list above. Although people achieve self-actualization in their own unique way, they tend to share certain characteristics. However, self-actualization is a matter of degree, 'There are no perfect human beings' (Maslow,1970a, p. 176).

It is not necessary to display all 15 characteristics to become self-actualized, and not only self-actualized people will display them. Maslow did not e□uate self-actualization with perfection. Self-actualization merely involves achieving one's potential. Thus, someone can be silly, wasteful, vain and impolite, and still self-actualize. Less than two percent of the population achieve self-actualization.

Educational applications

Maslow's (1968) hierarchy of needs theory has made a major contribution to teaching and classroom management in schools. Rather than reducing behavior to a response in the environment, Maslow (1970a) adopts a holistic approach to education and learning. Maslow looks at the complete physical, emotional, social, and intellectual □ualities of an individual and how they impact on learning.

Applications of Maslow's hierarchy theory to the work of the classroom teacher are obvious. Before a student's cognitive needs can be met they must first fulfil their basic physiological needs. For example a tired and hungry student will find it difficult to focus on learning. Students need to feel emotionally and physically safe and accepted within the classroom to progress and reach their full potential.

Maslow suggests students must be shown that they are valued and respected in the classroom and the teacher should create a supportive environment. Students with a low self-esteem will not progress academically at an optimum rate until their self-esteem is strengthened.

Critical evaluation

The most significant limitation of Maslow's theory concerns his methodology. Maslow formulated the characteristics of self-actualized individuals from undertaking a qualitative method called biographical analysis.

He looked at the biographies and writings of 18 people he identified as being self-actualized. From these sources he developed a list of qualities that seemed characteristic of this specific group of people, as opposed to humanity in general.

From a scientific perspective there are numerous problems with this particular approach. First, it could be argued that biographical analysis as a method is extremely subjective as it is based entirely on the opinion of the researcher. Personal opinion is always prone to bias, which reduces the validity of any data obtained. Therefore Maslow's operational definition of self-actualization must not be blindly accepted as scientific fact.

Furthermore, Maslow's biographical analysis focused on a biased sample of self-actualized individuals, prominently limited to highly educated white males (such as Thomas Jefferson, Abraham Lincoln, Albert Einstein, William James, Aldous Huxley, Gandhi, Beethoven).

Although Maslow (1970) did study self-actualized females, such as Eleanor Roosevelt and Mother Teresa, they comprised a small proportion of his sample. This makes it difficult to generalize his theory to females and individuals from lower social classes or different ethnicity. Thus questioning the population validity of Maslow's findings.

Furthermore, it is extremely difficult to empirically test Maslow's concept of self-actualization in a way that causal relationships can be established.

Another criticism concerns Maslow's assumption that the lower needs must be satisfied before a person can achieve their potential and self-actualize. This is not always the case, and therefore Maslow's hierarchy of needs in some aspects has been falsified.

Through examining cultures in which large numbers of people live in poverty (such as India) it is clear that people are still capable of higher order needs such as love and belongingness. However, this should not occur, as according to Maslow, people who have difficulty achieving very basic physiological needs (such as food, shelter etc.) are not capable of meeting higher growth needs.

Also, many creative people, such as authors and artists (e.g. Rembrandt and Van Gogh) lived in poverty throughout their lifetime, yet it could be argued that they achieved self-actualization.

Psychologists now conceptualize motivation as a pluralistic behavior, whereby needs can operate on many levels simultaneously. A person may be motivated by higher growth needs at the same time as lower level deficiency needs.

Contemporary research by Tay & Diener (2011) has tested Maslow's theory by analyzing the data of 60,865 participants from 123 countries, representing every major region of the world. The survey was conducted from 2005 to 2010.

Respondents answered questions about six needs that closely resemble those in Maslow's model: basic needs (food, shelter); safety; social needs (love, support); respect; mastery; and autonomy. They also rated their well-being across three discrete measures: life evaluation (a person's view of his or her life as a whole), positive feelings (day-to-day instances of joy or pleasure), and negative feelings (everyday experiences of sorrow, anger, or stress).

The results of the study support the view that universal human needs appear to exist regardless of cultural differences. However, the ordering of the needs within the hierarchy was not correct.

"Although the most basic needs might get the most attention when you don't have them" you don't need to fulfill them in order to get benefits [from the others]." Even when we are hungry, for instance, we can be happy with our friends. "They're like vitamins," Diener says about how the needs work independently. "We need them all."

Have a plan - The first step for handling any emergency disaster is a plan. Having this plan discussed, organized and in place beforehand is vital for smoothly handling something that can be sudden and definitely unexpected. Your plan can include emergency evacuation routes, meeting places, emergency numbers and what to do in case of separation. It can include who is responsible for what, locations of important information and places and step-by-step instructions for disaster preparations.

Safe location - Depending on where you live, having a safe location to go can mean a few different things. For some it may be an attic - high about the flood waters. For others it may be a basement - safe from the effects of a tornado. Discuss with your family members the safest place to go during a natural disaster and make sure everyone is clear as to where that place is. It is also important to discuss a common meeting place in case separation occurs.

First Aid - Stocking your home with the necessary first aid e□uipment can potentially mean the difference between life and death when it comes to a natural disaster. When disaster strikes, you may not have the ability to make it to the emergency room or even to the store for necessary first aid supplies. Be sure to have a well stocked medicine cabinet with all of the pain relievers, bandages and antiseptics you may need in the case of an emergency.

Food Storage - At the first sign of a disaster, people flock to the grocery stores to stock up on essentials that may be needed in case they become stranded in their home. This not only means that there will be a huge crowd rushing to your local grocery store, but supplies will quickly run out. Being prepared for such a situation is absolutely crucial. Consider building up your food storage with water, powdered milk, canned meats, beans and fruits and easy to prepare meals such as pasta, soups, etc.

Natural Disaster Control - When disaster strikes, it is important to have the supplies necessary to protect your home and property from the devastation effects of Mother Nature. In the case of a severe storm or tsunami, stormwater control measures can be (and should be) thought out and organized prior to a natural disaster occurring. This not only helps you feel better prepared, but will allow you to act ⬜uickly and assist you in better protecting your family, home and possessions.

Any kind of natural disaster may come unexpected. When they hit hard on your area, they create a major disruption in living. Power supply may shut down. If your short on food, you cannot just go out and shop in the market. Sometimes, communication lines are even cut-off. You have no choice but stay within your homes and keep your family secured until things outside has simmered down.

Your home may be your only shield against these disasters. For this, it is important that you keep it disaster-proof. You have to do this to lessen the impact of the disaster. You want to make sure you have all options to ensure safety and survival of your family, if in case things go crazy.

Disaster Preparedness Tips

The number one goal during disasters is to ensure safety. Disasters choose no one to harm. Once you become vulnerable, you may get hurt in an instant or worse, lose your life. But if you have a properly built disaster-proof home, you can always withstand the devastation.

To make this possible, you have to prepare your homes for it. Here's how:

1. Fix everything at home. Electrical wires that are left hanging and defective should be repaired and put back into its place.

Any leak in your pipe connection, especially your gas pipes should be checked in advance. If your roof is leaking, it should also be fixed and kept in good condition all the time. You may have to brace the roof using hurricane straps, to prevent it from being blown away.

2. Anything dangling on walls, especially with pointed edges, should be removed and stored away. Shelves and other fixtures should be fastened properly. Anchor heavy, huge and movable items in your home. Water heaters should be strapped to the wall or secured on the floor.

3. Fire-proof your home. Prepare the extinguishers and other fire safety tools. However, keep them out of the way but place them in accessible areas. Hide flammable materials and products and make sure they are far from any heat sources. Also, keep first aid kits within your reach. If worse goes to worst, design an evacuation plan.

4. Permanent shutters for the windows should be working. If you don't have none of this, it's best to find an alternative plan to protect the glass.

5. Anything obstructing should be removed. Branches of trees that are weak, should be cut off to prevent being blown away by strong winds. Reinforce your garage and make sure nothing is blocking it. In case, you may have to evacuate, you can drive away easily.

6. Do not make any permanent barring. If you want to escape safely in your homes, you need to keep your keys to unlock doors safely. You do not want to be trapped in case of fires.

Always be prepared. Don't wait for the last minute in finding solution on how to protect your family and your home. Protect your homes from natural disasters. It is for your advantage.

Since some tornados strike at night and come on ⬜uickly without much notice, it's a good thing to own a weather radio, which will send out both a warning tone and message when there are severe weather warnings and watches.

Top Five Tips for Building an Emergency Supply Kit (According to the American Red Cross):

- To keep a three-day supply of water in your home you need four quarts of water per day per person (two ⬜uarts for drinking and two ⬜uarts for food preparation and sanitation).
- Store foods that are ready to eat and that need no refrigeration or cooking. Look for canned fruits and veggies, high protein/high energy foods and food for infants if necessary. Also include in your stores some comfort foods.
- Have a first aid kit in your home and in each car including pain relievers, antacids, laxatives and anti-diarrhea medications.
- Tools such as tape, matches, containers, whistles, maps, flashlights, eating utensils and dishes, pliers and wrenches and flares are also important.
- A complete change of clothes and footwear for each person including extra diapers and blankets for infants and young children.

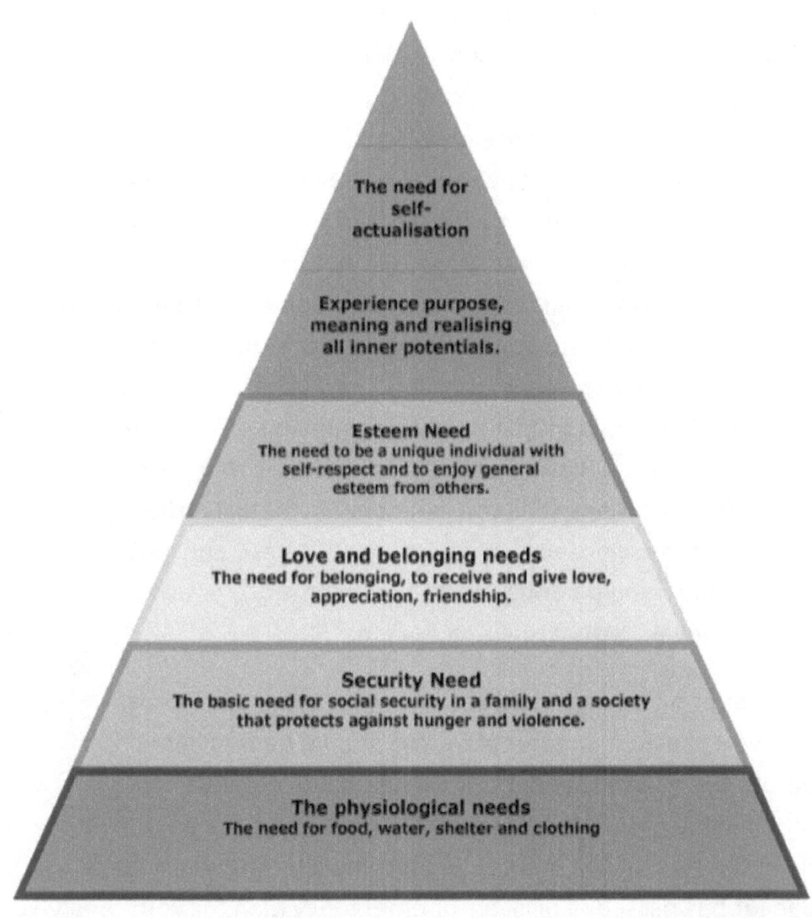

Needs at the bottom of the pyramid are basic physical requirements including the need for food, water, sleep and warmth. Once these lower-level needs have been met, people can move on to the next level of needs, which are for safety and security. As people progress up the pyramid, needs become increasingly psychological and social. Soon, the need for love, friendship and intimacy become important. Further up the pyramid, the need for personal esteem and feelings of accomplishment become important. Like Carl Rogers, Maslow emphasized the importance of self-actualization, which is a process of growing and developing as a person to achieve individual potential. At the University of Hawaii's Psychology Department website, I was reminded that Maslow was a humanistic psychologist. Humanists do not believe that human beings are pushed and pulled by mechanical forces, either of stimuli and reinforcements (behaviorism) or of unconscious instinctual impulses (psychoanalysis). Humanists focus upon potentials. They believe that humans strive for an upper level of capabilities. Humans seek the frontiers of creativity, the highest reaches of consciousness and wisdom. This has been labeled "fully functioning person", "healthy personality", or as Maslow calls this level, "self-actualizing person." .

One common thread you'll see in almost every section below is that you'll need a disaster plan. You should be familiar with it before the disaster, and ready to act on it in case the unthinkable happens. We can tell you all about the best thing to do in the heat of the moment—and we will—but when the danger has passed, a disaster or emergency plan for your family or coworkers can be the difference between you meeting up in a secure location or being lost, unable to find one another.

Keep your family's most important documents, like birth certificates, passports, and social security cards in a safe place in case you need to grab them and leave the house. Create a home inventory and keep it with those documents. Make digital copies, and put them on a flash drive in the same place. A portable safe/fireproof box is a good idea.

Make sure you have a well-stocked go-bag that will keep you safe, warm, fed, and any medical needs you have taken care of for at least a few days. Include things like emergency food and water, an emergency radio, batteries, extras of any prescriptions you take, and even a charged cell phone just for 911 purposes. 72hours's guide says that you should prepare to take care of yourself for at least 72 hours without help. If you want to plan for longer, this list is a good start.

Make sure you and your family have a planned and practiced escape route from your home, and a place you all agree to meet up if something terrible happens. Whether it's a disaster or a fire, everyone in your home should know the fastest way out of the house safely. Escape ladders from high windows are good investments, but if you live in an apartment building or high-rise, memorize the fastest route to a stairwell. Finally, practice your escape route with your family so everyone's clear on it.

Make sure you're familiar with the emergency or disaster plan at your office. Your company should have evacuation routes from your workplace and meet-up locations outside of the building. If you don't know what they are, ask. If no one knows what they are, come up with them on your own. Ask yourself where the closest stairwell to your desk or work area is, and time yourself getting to it. Find out where the closest first-aid kit in the office is, in case you need it.

Gear and kits are great, and you should definitely have them on hand, but nothing replaces a good escape plan that you can quickly act on without thinking about it in case of an emergency. Many people die in accidents and natural disasters simply because they don't know what to do and find themselves waiting for someone to tell them. Plan accordingly.

Prepare an emergency supplies kit to ride out any event. Downloadable lists of suggested kit contents and disaster protection devices are available on the FLASH site (search "disaster kit"). FLASH's Chapman-Henderson recommends buying only products that are tested and approved to a national or certified testing standard.

Among items to include:

• A radio capable of receiving NOAA Weather Radio All Hazards transmissions available on seven VHF fre uencies from 162.400 MHz to 162.550 MHz. Remember extra batteries.

• A First Aid kit that includes such items as a first-aid manual, antiseptic wipes, antibiotic cream, sharp scissors, and tweezers. Include prescription medications, including those for your pet.

• Water. Have about a gallon per person and pet per day. Stock enough for at least three days. Include extra water for sanitation.

• Nonperishable food and the all-important manual can opener. Have enough food for at least three days. Don't forget pet food.

• Flashlights, extra batteries, and portable chargers for cellphones and such. Charge all cell phones and PDAs the night before any storm is due.

• Garbage bags.

• Matches in a waterproof container.

• Personal hygiene products and moist towelettes.

10 ways a disaster could affect you: the real reasons you should prepare

Disasters can affect you and your family in many more ways than you think. Here are some of the compelling reasons why you should get prepared for disasters and emergencies.

We know what happens in emergencies like a bushfire, flood or cyclone. We see it in the media every year: dramatic images of houses ablaze, rooftops being torn away by raging winds, floodwaters carrying away everything in their path. We've seen what happens

Or have we?

Research has shown that the true cost of natural disasters is 50 per cent greater than previously estimated. So what's the reason for this?

It's the long-term impact disasters have on people: the psychological and social consequences that are often hidden from view. Here are some of the ways you can be affected by a disaster, and some steps to help you get prepared.

The loss of life

While no one likes to talk about it, emergencies can cause loss of life. Think about the impact that the death of a family member would have on your life and what impact your own death would have on those around you. Think not only about the emotional impacts, but also the practical ones. Not having a will can cause significant emotional and financial stress for surviving family members. If you haven't already, consider making a will and organising life insurance - it will help your family should the worst happen.

The loss of your house and irreplaceable possessions.

Homes can be damaged and destroyed in emergencies, large or small. Think about how you might protect your home. Ask your state fire and emergency services for information to help you protect your home from bushfires, floods, cyclones and other hazards.

Objects can shape our identity. Saving precious items and keepsakes can speed up the recovery process because it protects the links we have with the past and can bring significant comfort if we've lost property and/or loved ones. Think about all the important items in your life that might cause distress if they were lost.

The stress of being separated from your family

Being separated from family and friends is one of the most stressful things a person can experience when disaster strikes. Not knowing where your loved ones are or being unable to get a hold of them adds to that anxiety - especially if the usual communication lines are down. Deciding on an emergency meeting point or out-of-town contact with your family can help with that stress. If you need to, use a service like Register. Find. Reunite. if you want to find out about friends and family during a disaster or let them know you're OK.

The loss of your job and income

It's not just that emergencies can be financially costly - they can also cost you your job. Think about how your ability to earn an income might be affected by an emergency. Your workplace

might close down due to damage, cleaning up damaged
property may re□uire time off work, and sometimes you'll need
to take sick leave for illness or injury suffered as a result of the
emergency. Have you prepared adequate income insurance in
case of unemployment?

Financial hardship

Emergencies can be really expensive and financial matters can
become a significant burden that causes a lot of stress to
people. Think about how you can plan to cover financial losses
caused by an emergency and in doing so avoid the stressful
burden that accessing money can become. While there might
be financial assistance available from governments and other
agencies after an emergency, it's usually small and targeted at
immediate needs. It won't be enough to replace your home or
valuables. Thinking about how you can cover financial losses
caused by an emergency will save you a lot of stress and
burden.

Your physical health

As a result of the stress experienced in the aftermath of an
emergency, you may well neglect your health and wellbeing.
Research has shown that natural disasters can worsen chronic
disease. It could be from illness caused by the disaster, or
separation from medication or treatment due to the disruption
- especially in rural and remote areas. If you have an illness or
chronic condition, make sure you make a plan for this in case of
an emergency. It's important to maintain a healthy lifestyle, as
much as possible to help manage the stress of recovery.

Your mental health

Really stressful events can affect the way our brains work. Many people talk about experiencing memory loss, losing the ability to concentrate, and finding it hard to read and retain information after an emergency. This is common. Other ways disasters can impact your mental health include post traumatic stress disorder, depression or anxiety, all of which can have serious implications to other aspects of your life.

Your family and relationships

The stress and hardships of experiencing a disaster can have negative conse□uences on your relationships and family life. Unfortunately, research and experience tell us that family violence increases in the often chaotic circumstances after an emergency, as living arrangements and support networks are disrupted.

Family violence can include physical, sexual, emotional, verbal, social and/ or spiritual violence. Think about how you and others might manage challenging situations - such as pre-existing apprehended violence orders and custody arrangements - after an emergency. If you're worried about family violence occurring after an emergency, talk to your personal support network, family violence services or the police.

Your children

Emergencies impact children and infants just as much as adults. Most parents worry about these impacts, and often see changes in behaviour after an emergency. For most kids, the way their parents cope will be the strongest indication of how they will cope. It's important to understand the common reactions that

children have after a disaster. Find out how you can help
children cope with a disaster.

Disruption to your community and social networks

An emergency can cause serious upheaval to your community,
and this means the loss of friends, neighbours and your social
networks and pastimes such as clubs or sports teams. This can
leave people feeling isolated and lacking the support they might
need. Even a smaller scale disaster, like a house fire, can mean
temporarily moving to a new area with unfamiliar faces, making
the recovery process even more difficult. Strong communities
before an emergency have been shown to be strong after the
emergency, providing much needed support from within. Take
steps to build your community links. It's as easy as opening the
door, or exchanging phone numbers.

The loss of your local heritage and environment

Places can provide us with a sense of who we are and a
connection to our community, with landscapes and landmarks
making our world familiar. Loss of, or damage to, these can
have profound effects on people, both practically, in terms of
physical disorientation, and in terms of impacting links to
people's pasts and their identities. While there is not a lot you
can do about this, photographing those buildings, landmarks
and landscapes can help.

Preparing for the psychological effects of disaster and emergencies

It's not just about buildings: disasters and emergencies will affect you in many more ways than you think. Whether its stress, financial hardship or upheaval to your community, they all have a serious effect on your wellbeing that will make recovering harder. For some people, it can take years to fully recover from a disaster.

So in addition to taking practical action to protect your property, remember that it's just as important to prepare for the emotional toll disasters can take so you can get your life back on track.

Get prepared for disasters and emergencies

Emergencies can happen at any time. They could be as large as a bushfire or as personal as a death in the family. And an emergency can disrupt your life in ways you don't expect. You could experience stress and anxiety, relationship problems and financial hardships, often for years to come. Being prepared makes it much easier for you to recover.

Off Grid Living

Find a location with adequate resources. When you go off the grid, you are removing yourself from mainstream society. You will be fending for yourself, gathering food and water and providing your own shelter. You won't have access to public utilities and other services that you get living in a regular community.

Find a place that can offer you enough resources, including food supply, water supply, and shelter.

You may be able to adapt a cabin for your own purposes, or you might want to build yourself a new house or cabin.

You might choose a location that is a couple of hours' drive from the nearest gas station or grocery store. There may be no hospital within many miles. If this is the case, you might not have access to medical services.

Get your energy sources squared away. You no longer have electricity from the local power company, so if you want electricity, you will need to find a way to produce your own. Solar and water power will allow you to use lights, refrigerator, washing machine, music player, and other machines.

Look into purchasing additional solar panels as you can afford them. While you might adjust to life with less electricity, there are certain conveniences that you will probably want.

Get rechargeable batteries. Make sure they are never less than 50% charged to ensure that you will always have enough power.

Have access to a filtered water supply. If you do not have access to town water, you may need to sink a well in order to meet your water needs. If you choose to build your own well, you might need a permit, depending on your state. Be sure to stay at least 50 feet away from any septic tank, marshy areas and any other areas with potential contamination.

Use a water-testing kit. This kit will help you determine whether your water has safe or unsafe levels of certain chemicals in it. These kits are readily available online or at home improvement stores. Some counties offer free water testing as well.

Be sure to filter your water to avoid sickness. For example, if your water is high in lime, you may get a stomach ache if you drink it unfiltered.

Have medical supplies handy. If your location is so remote that the nearest hospital is more than an hour or two away, you should consider becoming knowledgeable of simple medical procedures.

Assemble a medical kit with supplies such as bandages, antibiotics, penicillin, thread and needle for doing stitches, and other supplies.

The10 min DIY water distillery: Using two, one liter clear soda bottles. Put 1/4 inch holes in both caps, insert 1/4 inch clear tubing thru each cap and down into each bottle (about 5-7 feet of tubing). Secure each cap onto bottles. Fill one 3/4 with water you want to distill, bring tubing about 1/2 inch from top. place in sunlight. Bring the tubing to the bottom of other bottle and place it in shade. As the sun heats up the water and the water goes into a gas, expanding and going into the bottle in shade, it cools down and turns back into water, filling the bottle in shade, with clear drinkable water. This can also be used to remove salt from saltwater. Place a black band of tape around the input bottle, making sure not to mix them up.

Start a garden. While you might have food occasionally delivered to your off-grid location, you also need to provide food for yourself. Plant a large garden with a variety of vegetables.

Learn what plants can grow in different seasons so that you constantly have fresh food growing in your garden.

Store vegetables over the winter. Potatoes, onions, carrots and other root vegetables are especially well-suited to long-term storage in a cool place.

Get a few livestock animals. If you have cows or goats of both sexes, you can be provided with meat and milk, depending on the breed. Chickens and ducks can provide meat and eggs.

Figure out if you need to generate income. If you have a lot of savings, you might be able to go off the grid without needing to continue working. But if you don't have substantial savings, you will probably still need to generate income in some way. Think about sources for income, including selling vegetables or artisan craft items at a nearby farmer's market.

If you're off the grid, your internet access may be limited or nonexistent. This might make telecommuting a difficult proposition.

Handling Being Alone

Express lonely feelings. If you are starting to feel lonely after cutting yourself off, don't bottle up those feelings. Express them through creative outlets, such as journaling, painting, dancing or singing.

Get a pet. Research shows that pets can improve your mood and your overall health. A person with a pet will likely have lower blood pressure and lower indicators of heart disease, such as triglyceride and cholesterol levels, Having a companion such as a cat or dog can ease loneliness as well.

Take up a hobby. Keep your mind busy with a stimulating activity. Hobbies keep you moving forward. They can also help you with focus and concentration. Find a hobby that you like, such as knitting, playing music, gardening or woodworking.

Participate in a solo sport. Just because you've cut yourself off from society doesn't mean you have to spend your time holed up in your house. Get outside and get some exercise by participating in a solo sport, like cycling, hiking, running, or yoga

Terrorizem and how to suvive

While people may consider the shootings at Sandy Hook and Aurora to be terrorist attacks, by definition, they were not. In fact, according to the Federal Bureau of Investigation (FBI), "there is no single, universally accepted, definition of terrorism. Terrorism is defined in the Code of Federal Regulations as 'the unlawful use of force and violence against persons or property to intimidate or coerce a government, the civilian population, or any segment thereof, in furtherance of political or social objectives.'" It is difficult to be fully prepared for something when it's not clear exactly what it is that you're preparing for.

Along with the FBI, the Federal Emergency Management Agency (FEMA) also has provided some general terrorism information:

Acts of Terrorism

• threats of terrorism

• assassinations

• kidnappings

• hijackings

- bomb scares and bombings

- cyber attacks (computer-based)

- the use of chemical, biological, nuclear, and radiological weapons

High-Risk Targets for Acts of Terrorism

- military and civilian government facilities

- international airports

- large cities

- high-profile landmarks

- large public gatherings

- water and food supplies

- utilities

- corporate centers

- mailings (explosives or chemical/biological agents may be sent through the mail)

The Seven Signs of Terrorism

Fearing future terrorist attacks does not mean that people have to live in fear every day. There are several steps people may take to help prepare and protect their families. One such action is to become familiar with the Seven Signs of Terrorism, developed by the Metropolitan Transportation Authority of New York, that have been adopted by State Police across the country as an educational tool.

1. **Surveillance**: Be on the lookout for someone recording or monitoring activities. The type of recording does not have to be as obvious as a camera or a video camera; the person may be taking notes, drawing diagrams, annotating maps, or using binoculars, etc.

2. **Elicitation:** Be wary of people or groups who attempt to learn information about military operations, capabilities, or people. The attempts do not have to be face-to-face. They may be made by mail, telephone, etc.

3. **Tests of Security:** If someone is attempting to evaluate the strengths and weaknesses of security measures, or if he is attempting to record and analyze reaction times to security breaches, contact your local authorities.

4. **Acquiring Supplies**: Be vigilant about people who purchase or steal explosives, weapons, ammunition, etc. Other supplies that may be needed for a terrorist attack are military uniforms, flight manuals, badges or the equipment to make them, and any other controlled items. And, as we learned in the Boston bombing, materials such as pressure cookers and fireworks also may be supplies that terrorists purchase in large quantities.

5. **Suspicious persons out of place**: Of course, we are wary of people who don't seem to belong in our neighborhoods. But, people also may arouse suspicion at work, businesses, or anywhere, for that matter. Also be alert for people who suspiciously cross the border, stow away on board a ship, or jump ship in port if you are traveling.

6. **Dry run/Trial run**: Terrorists may practice their attack prior to carrying it out, so watch for people who move around but don't seem to have a true purpose. A terrorist also may map out

routes or time traffic lights, so be on the lookout for these types of activities.

7. **Deploying Assets**: Terrorists have to get people and supplies positioned prior to committing the terrorist act. If you suspect these activities are occurring, immediately contact the authorities because this may be the last chance you have to do so before the terrorist act takes place.

Virtually all state and federal agencies encourage families to take the time to prepare for terrorist attacks. There are three steps to help you get started on protecting your loved ones from acts of terrorism:

Know your work, school, and community disaster plans. If you do not know the plans, contact your supervisor, school administrators, or local fire department for information.

Identify an alternative hospital. Hospitals closest to the event always are the busiest.

Use online resources to create disaster plans and review steps for protecting yourself and your loved ones. FEMA provides a downloadable Family Emergency Plan.

Terrorist Attack: In a Public Place

Terrorists typically attack public places with large crowds because they want to cause the most damage and get the most attention for their cause. One of the best ways to keep your family safe from terrorist attacks in public places is to share and discuss the Seven Signs of Terrorism with age-appropriate children.

public

A simpler way to discuss the signs of terrorism with children is to focus on "Look and Listen." This approach narrows the Seven Signs of Terrorism to a more kid-friendly version that includes looking for:

- bags left unattended in public places.
- people checking areas or buildings.
- people trying to enter secure areas.
- people at events wearing too much clothing.

Terrorist Attack: Explosive Devices

Terrorists use explosive devices as one of their most common weapons. According to a report by the National Consortium for the Study of Terrorism and Responses to Terrorism, bombings/explosions account for 51.53% of the tactics used in terrorist attacks in the United States from 1970-2011.

Unfortunately, information for making explosive devices is readily available online and in other information sources, and the materials necessary for making the explosives easily are found in many places. Because of the portable nature of explosive devices and the ease with which they may be detonated from remote locations, terrorists rely on this type of weapon fre uently.

One way to keep your family safe from these explosive devices is to know which types of parcels are suspect. Look for parcels that:

- are unexpected or from someone unknown to you

- have no return address, or have one that can't be verified
- are marked with restrictions such as "Personal," "Confidential," or "Do not X-ray"
- have protruding wires or aluminum foil, strange odors, or stains
- show a city or state in the postmark that doesn't match the return address
- are an unusual weight for their size or are lopsided or oddly shaped
- are marked with threatening language
- have inappropriate or unusual labeling
- have excessive postage or packaging material such as masking tape or string
- have misspellings of common words
- are addressed to someone not at the address listed or are otherwise outdated
- have incorrect titles or titles without a name
- are not addressed to a specific person
- have hand-written or poorly typed addresses

Be proactive about checking packages and share the information with your age-appropriate children. They may be responsible for getting your mail after school, or they may love to pick up the boxes left on your stoop during the day, so it is important that they know which types of packages may be unsafe. Of course, if you or your loved ones suspect a parcel for any reason, do not touch it, leave the area, and immediately contact local authorities. It is always best to alert authorities, even if you are unsure whether there is a true danger.

Protective Measures for an Explosion

Because most bombings occur in public places, your family should know what to do in the event of an explosion. As with any emergency drill, parents should practice the following tips with age-appropriate children and discuss what to do in the event of being trapped in or being near the scene of a bombing. Remember, the goal is to empower your children with knowledge, not to frighten them.

If your family is trapped in debris, you should:

- use a flashlight to signal your location to rescuers, if possible.
- avoid unnecessary movement so you don't stir the dust.
- cover your nose and mouth with some sort of material that is nearby, to breathe through. Dense-weave cotton material acts as a good filter, or you may wet the material before breathing through it to help filter the dust.
- tap on a pipe or wall so rescuers can hear where you are.
- use a whistle to signal rescuers, if possible.
- shout as a last resort, only. Shouting can cause you to inhale dangerous amount of dust.

If your family is near the scene of an explosion, you should:

- get under a sturdy table or desk if things are falling around you. When the items stop falling, leave quickly. Watch for obviously weakened floors and stairways,

and be especially vigilant about falling debris. Do not
use elevators.

- follow your family, job, or school emergency disaster
  plan for leaving and staying away from the explosion.
  Do not stop to retrieve personal possessions or make
  any calls or texts. Do not return to the scene because
  you will increase the risk of danger for rescue workers
  and your family.
- avoid crowds. Crowds of people may be the target of a
  second attack.
- avoid unattended cars and trucks, as these may contain
  explosives.
- do not stand in front of windows, glass doors, or other
  potentially dangerous areas, including damaged
  buildings. Move at least 10 blocks or 200 yards away
  from damaged buildings. Also remember to move away
  from sidewalks or streets that will be used by
  emergency officials or other people still exiting the
  building.
- follow directions from people in authority, including
  police, fire, EMS, military personnel, school supervisors,
  or workplace supervisors.
- call 911 once you are in a safe place, but only if police,
  fire, or EMS has not arrived to help injured people.
- help others who are hurt or need assistance to leave
  the area if you are able to do so. If you see someone
  who is seriously injured, seek help. Do not attempt to
  manage the situation alone.
- listen to your radio or television for news and
  instructions.

Terrorist Attack: Biological, Chemical, or Nuclear Attacks

Keeping your family safe from a biological, chemical, or nuclear attack requires more specific preparations, as you may need to remain in your home in the event of one of these attacks. It may be too late to obtain the materials necessary to keep your family safe after one of these types of attacks occurs, so FEMA has created checklists for families to do before these threats arise:

Protecting Yourself, Your Family, and Your Property

- Build an Emergency Supply Kit. Include nonperishable food, water, a battery-powered radio, extra flashlights, and batteries.
- For a chemical threat, also have a roll of duct tape and scissors in your Emergency Supply Kit, as well as plastic for doors, windows, and vents for the room in which you will be sheltered. Premeasure and cut the plastic sheeting for each opening.
- For a nuclear threat, increase your disaster supplies to be adequate for up to two weeks, during periods of heightened threat.
- Make a Family Emergency Plan. Your family should know how to contact one another because it is possible that you will not all be together at the time of an attack. You should know how to get back together and what to do in the case of an emergency.
- Plan meeting places, both within and outside of your neighborhood.
- Designate an out-of-town contact number because local numbers may be unavailable.

- Be familiar with emergency plans at work, daycare centers, and schools where your family spends time. If no plans are in place, volunteer to help create one.
- Know your community's warning systems and disaster plans.
- For a nuclear threat, know your community's evacuation routes. Ask local officials if any public buildings have been designated as fallout shelters. If none has been designated, make your own list of potential shelters near your home, workplace, and school. These would include basements or the windowless center area of middle floors in high-rise buildings, as well as subways and tunnels. If you live in an apartment building or high-rise, talk to the manager about the safest place in the building for shelter and about providing for building occupants until it is safe to go out.
- Notify caregivers and babysitters about your plan.
- Make plans for your pets.
- For a chemical threat, choose an internal room for shelter. One without windows and on the highest level of your home is best.
- Check with your doctor to be sure all immunizations are up to date. Children and older adults are especially vulnerable to biological agents.
- Consider installing a High-Efficiency Particulate Air (HEPA) filter in your furnace return duct. These filters remove particles in the air and will filter out most biological agents that may enter your house. If you do not have a central heating or cooling system, a portable HEPA filter can be used.

General Guidelines for Preparing for a Terrorist Attack

- Be aware of your surroundings.
- Move or leave if you feel uncomfortable or if your instincts tell you something is not right.
- Take precautions when traveling.
- Be aware of conspicuous or unusual behavior.
- Do not accept packages from strangers.
- Do not leave your luggage unattended.
- Immediately report unusual behavior, suspicious or unattended packages, and strange devices to police or security.
- Know where emergency exits are located in buildings that you fre□uently visit. Plan how to get out if an emergency arises.
- Be prepared to function without services you typically rely on, including electricity, telephone, cell phone service, natural gas, gasoline pumps, cash registers, ATMs, and Internet transactions.
- If you work or live in a large building, work with building owners or managers to be sure the following items are located on each floor of the building:
- Portable, battery-operated radio with extra batteries
- Several flashlights and extra batteries
- First aid kits and manual
- Hard hats and dust masks
- Fluorescent tape to rope off dangerous areas

The unfortunate reality is that there have already been numerous terrorist attacks on U.S. soil. And there will be more. With counter-terrorism measures advancing every day, the hope is that our technology is capable of predicting attacks and even halting terrorists in their tracks. Preparing for a terrorist attack, and devising a response plan for various scenarios, is the best way to keep your family safe.

How to protect yourself from Ebola

Emergency services are gearing themselves up for an Ebola outbreak in the UK - so we have put together 10 steps you could take to avoid catching it

As direct flights from Britain to Sierra Leone are cancelled over Ebola fears and as concerns of an outbreak in the UK grow, Mirror Online looks at how you can protect yourself from the disease.

Ebola is spread by contact with the fluids of someone who is infected – including saliva, sweat, blood, vomit and urine.

So far - no vaccine or cure is available.

Most of Ebola's 4,300 victims have come from West Africa but medical experts say the UK should be prepared.

Stay clean: Doctors recommend you should always keep your hands clean (Image: Getty)

According to the Centre for Disease Control and Prevention, you should wash your hands thoroughly with warm water and soap. Alcohol-based hand sanitizers can be used as an alternative.

Avoid contact with anyone you believe is infected

Health care workers wait for the arrival of a possible Ebola patient at the Texas Health Presbyterian Hospital

Mask up: Dress in protective clothing and avoid shaking hands with any patients (Image: Getty)

This should go without saying, but in particular avoid their bodily fluids. Don't shake hands, either.

And should you need to go near someone with Ebola you need to be wearing protective gear, including a face mask and gloves.

Those blokes that boarded the plane when a passenger claimed to have Ebola? That's the get up that you need. You can buy something similar from Amazon. Yes, really.

Disinfect any potentially infected areas

Clean up: It's important to disinfect all items of clothes and bedding (Image: Julian Hamilton / Daily Mirror)

The World Health Organisation says any areas an infected person could have had contact with - like bed linens - should be disinfected.

Know the warning signs

Staff from North East Ambulance Service and the Royal Victoria Infirmary, Newcastle take part in a national exercise to test Britain's readiness for an Ebola outbreak

Get to hospital: Staff in Britain are being trained in how to cope with an outbreak

A sudden temperature, muscle aches, vomiting or a rash might indicate you have the disease.

Diarrhoea, stomach pain, unexplained bruising or bleeding and loss of appetite can also be warning signs.

Know what to do

If you think someone has been infected, or if you think you might have Ebola, the best thing to do is isolate yourself and call medical help immediately.

Do not touch bats, chimpanzees, gorillas or monkeys

Don't touch: No matter how cute monkeys are - keep your distance

Or their blood or fluids. And do not eat raw meat prepared from these animals. Scientists believe this is how the disease first transmitted to humans.

Avoid dead bodies

If you think someone has died from Ebola, do not touch their body. You can still catch Ebola from their body as it emits fluids that make it even more contagious than that of a sick person.

Avoid travelling to affected countries

William Pooley beat Ebola but you might not be so lucky

The Department of Transport cited the deteriorating public health situation for cancelling flights to Sierra Leone.

It's probably best to take that advice on board.

Treat injuries

Any sorts of cuts and bleeding injuries should not be exposed and should be kept covered. The virus can enter the body through open wounds.

Privacy

you probably know the feeling.

It's the early hours of the morning. You're in bed, but a strange feeling has wakened you. You sense a presence in your house. Cautiously, trying your utmost to be silent, you creep downstairs and peer into the gloom of your living room. A curtain is flapping in the breeze, broken glass sparkling on the moonlit floor. Something of yours — a TV, perhaps — is gone.

Almost everyone who has experienced property crime will tell you that the loss of physical things isn't the real blow. It's the sense that the sanctity of home and hearth has been "violated" that really hurts.

That could be happening to you right now, in the middle of the day, even as you sit alone in your comfortable home ... because if thieves aren't hacking into your house, they can too easily violate your privacy online.

Passwords Won't Secure Your Internet Privacy

The Centre for International Governance Innovation (CIGI) recently surveyed Internet users in 24 countries, and found that 64% of respondents are more worried about their privacy since Edward Snowden blew the lid on National Security Agency (NSA) spying. Large numbers of people are updating their passwords more frequently and avoiding websites and software that might put their data at risk.

If only that were enough. The CIGI report noted that more than 750 million people around the world have taken steps to improve their privacy since Snowmen's revelations … but that these steps would make "little difference to the NSA's ability to gather data on them or to defy the surveillance techniques of large firms."

Indeed, passwords are of little conse□uence to a determined hacker — especially one that isn't hacking into your computer, but rather into the mainframe of a company or government agency with whom you do business, where your password is stored along with millions of others.

Strong passwords are essential, of course, and regular changes to them are important. (Indeed, a password manager I use has recently added a feature that can change all of your passwords with one click.) But passwords can only protect you from garden-variety data theft. They're like burglar bars on your home — important, but once they're compromised, you're completely exposed. You need more than passwords to be truly secure.

Here are three ways to get started on a sound personal privacy strategy:

An Alarm System: Most reputable websites now have a feature that alerts you by email or text message or both whenever someone logs into your account. Such alerts can also be set for transactions above a certain amount. I've saved myself money on more than one occasion after getting such an alert and calling my bank immediately to stop the transaction … even while I've been overseas.

Play Your Cards Close to Your Chest: Every good poker player knows that the secret to success is to limit the information about you available to the other players. The same goes with digital security. Don't do business with websites or use "apps" that ask for more information than is reasonably required. This is especially true of "free" services that essentially want information about you so they can sell it to someone else. Don't participate in surveys, submit reviews or participate in other aspects of websites that aren't strictly necessary.

Encrypt, encrypt, encrypt: Above all, turn your data into a form that's useless to anyone who doesn't have the key to unlock its meaning. As I've stressed before and will surely do again, use solid encryption software and, where appropriate, a secure browsing setup like TOR. It's not that they are impossible to hack … but they are so hard to crack that almost all potential digital burglars will move on to another victim.

Do not reveal personal information inadvertently.

You may be "shedding" personal details, including e-mail addresses

and other contact information, without even knowing it unless you

properly configure your Web browser. In your browser's "Setup",

"Options" or "Preferences" menus, you may wish to use a pseudonym instead of your real name, and not enter an e-mail address, nor provide other personally identifiable

information that you don't wish to share. When visiting a site you

trust you can choose to give them your info, in forms on their site;

there is no need for your browser to potentially make this information

available to all comers. Also be on the lookout for system-wide

"Internet defaults" programs on your computer (some examples include

Window's Internet Control Panel, and MacOS's Configuration Manager,

and the third-party Mac utility named Internet Config). While they are useful

for various things, like keeping multiple Web browers and other

Internet tools consistent in how the treat downloaded files and such,

they should probably also be anonymized just like your browser itself,

if they contain any fields for personal information. Households with

children may have an additional "security problem" - have you set clear rules for your kids, so that they know not to reveal personal

information unless you OK it on a site-by-site basis?

Turn on cookie notices in your Web browser, and/or use cookie management software or infomediaries.

"Cookies" are tidbits of information that Web sites store on your

computer, temporarily or more-or-less permanently. In many cases

cookies are useful and inocuous. They may be passwords and user IDs,

so that you do not have to keep retyping them every time you load a

new page at the site that issued the cookie. Other cookies however, can be used for "data

mining" purposes, to track your motions through a Web site, the time

you spend there, what links you click on and other details that the

company wants to record, usually for marketing purposes. Most cookies

can only be read by the party that created them. However, some companies that manage online banner advertising are, in essence, cookie sharing rings. They

can track which pages you load, which ads you click on, etc., and share this information

with all of their client Web sites

Browsers are starting

to allow user control over cookies. Netscape, for example, allows you

to see a notice when a site tries to write a cookie file to your hard

drive, and gives you some information about it, allowing you to decide

whether or not to accept it. (Be on the lookout for cookies the

function of which is not apparent, which go to other sites than the one you are trying to load, or which

are not temporary). It also allows you to automatically block all

cookies that are being sent to third parties (or to block all cookies,

entirely, but this will make some sites inoperable). Internet

Explorer has a cookie management interface in addition to

Netscape-like features, allowing you to selectively enable or disable cookies on a site-by-site basis, even to allow cookies for a site

generally, but delete a specific cookie you are suspicious about. With

Internet Explorer you can also turn on cookies for a site temporarily

then disable them when you no longer need them (e.g., at an online

bookstore that requires cookies to process an order, but whom you

don't want to track what books you are looking at, what links you are

following, etc., the rest of the time.) Turning on cookie warnings

will cause alert boxes to pop up, but after some practice you may learn

to hit "Decline" so fast that you hardly notice them any more. The

idea is to only enable cookies on sites that require them AND whom you

trust.

There are also numerous "cookie eater" applications,

some which run on a schedule or in the background, that delete cookie files for you. As with turning off

cookies entirely, you may have trouble accessing sites that require certain cookies (though in most cases the worst that will happen is that you'll have to re-enter a login ID and password

you thought were saved.) "Eating" the cookies periodically still permits sites to track what

you're doing for a short time (i.e., the time between successive deletion of your cookie file),

but thwarts attempts to discern and record your actions over time.

Yet another option is to use an "infomediary" (some are home-use software products, others may be network-based services),

such as SeigeSoft's

SiegeSurfer (http://www.siegesoft.com/_html/tutorial.asp),

Zero Knowledge Systems' Freedom

(http://www.freedom.net), among others. These products/services act as a proxy or

shield between you and sites you visit, and can completely disguise to Web sites where you are coming from

and who you are (and intercept all cookies). Most are Windows-only at this point, though

Orangatango (http://www.orangatango.com/), and SafeWeb

and (http://www.safeweb.com) also offer

such services that are Web-based and not platform-dependent.

WARNING: Do not confuse honest infomediaries

with "identity managmenet services" like Microsoft's Passport service or Novell's DigitalMe. While you may gain some

temporary convenience at sites that support them, you'll lose essential privacy, because these services are not

there to serve you but to serve marketing purposes by collecting a vast array of information about you and selling it.

The best solution doesn't exist yet: Full cookie management abilities built

into the browsers themselves. Only increased user pressure on Microsoft, Netscape

and other browser makers can make this happen. Users should ultimately be able

to reject cookies on a whole-domain basis, reject all third-party cookies by default, reject all cookies that are not essential

for the transaction at hand, receive notice of exactly what a cookie is intended for,

and be able to set default behaviors and permissions rather than have to interact with cookies on a page-by-page

basis. This just isn't possible yet. You may wish to contact the company that makes your browser software and

demand these essential features in the next version.

Keep a "clean" e-mail address.

When mailing to unknown parties; posting to newsgroups, mailing

lists, chat rooms and other public spaces on the Net; or publishing a

Web page that mentions your e-mail address, it is best to do this from

a "side" account, some pseudonymous or simply alternate address, and

to use your main or preferred address only on small, members-only

lists and with known, trusted individuals. Addresses that are posted

(even as part of message headers) in public spaces can be easily

discovered by spammers (online junk mailers) and added to their list of

targets. If your public "throw away" address gets spammed enough to become

annoying, you can simply kill it off, and start a new one. Your

friends, boss, etc., will still know your "real" address. You can use

a free (advertising-supported) e-mail service provider like Yahoo Mail or Hotmail for such "side" accounts. It is best to use a "real"

Internet service provider for your main account, and to examine their

privacy policies and terms of service, as some "freemail" services may have

poor privacy track records. You may find it works best to use an

e-mail package that allows mulitiple user IDs and addresses (a.k.a.

"personalities", "aliases") so that you do not have to switch between multiple

programs to manange and use more than one e-mail address (though you may have to use a Web browser rather than an e-mail program to read your

mail in your "throw away" accounts - many freemail providers do not

allow POP or IMAP connections). If you are "required"

to give an e-mail address to use a site (but will not be required to

check your mail for some kind of access code they send you), you can

use "someuser@example.com" (example.com is a non-existent site,

set up by the Internet standards to be used as an example that will never accidentally coincide with anyone's real e-mail address, which

is always a danger if you just make up one off the top of your head.)

Don't reveal personal details to strangers or just-met

"friends".

The speed of Internet communication is often mirrored

in rapid online

acquaintanceships and friendships. But it is important to realize that

you don't really know who these people are or what they are like in

real life. A thousand miles away, you don't have friends-of-friends

or other references about this person. Be also wary of face-to-face

meetings. If you and your new e-friend wish to meet in person, do it

in a public place. Bringing a friend along can also be a good idea.

One needn't be paranoid, but one should not be an easy mark, either.

Some personal information you might wish to withhold until you know someone much better would include your full name, place of employment,

phone number, and street address (among more obvious things like

credit card numbers, etc.) Needless to say, such information should

not be put on personal home pages. (If you have a work home page, it

may well have work contact information on it, but you needn't reveal

this page to everyone you meet in a chat room.) For this and other

reasons, many people maintain two personal home pages, a work-related

one, and an "off duty" version. In the commercial sector, too, beware

"fast-met friends". A common

"social engineering"

form

of industrial espionage is to befriend someone online just long

enough to get them to reveal insider information.

Realize you may be monitored at work, avoid sending highly

personal e-mail to mailing lists, and keep sensitive files on your

home computer.

In most US states and many if not most countries, employees have little if any privacy protection

from monitoring by employers. When discussing sensitive matters in

e-mail or other online media, be certain

with whom you are communicating

. If you replied to a mailing list post, check the headers - is your reply

going to the person you think it is, or to the whole list? Also be

aware that an increasing number of employers are monitoring and

recording employee Web usage, as well as e-mail. This could compromise

home banking passwords and other sensitive information. Keep private

Beware sites that offer some sort of reward or prize in exchange for your contact information or other personal details

There's a very high probability that they are gathering this information for direct marketing purposes. In many cases your name and

address are worth much more to them because they can sell it to other

marketers (who can do the same in turn...) than what

you are (supposedly) getting from them. Be especially wary of

sweepstakes and contests. You probably won't win, but the marketer

sure will if you give them your information.

Do not reply to spammers, for any reason.

"Spam", or unsolicited bulk e-mail, is something you are probably

already familiar with (and tired of). If you get a spammed

advertisment, certainly don't take the sender up on whatever offer

they are making, but also don't bother replying with "REMOVE" in the

subject line, or whatever (probably bogus) unsubscribe instructions

you've been given). This simply confirms that your address is being

read by a real person, and you'll find yourself on dozens more

spammers' lists in no time. If you open the message, watch your outgoing mail queue to make sure that a "return receipt" message was

not generated to be sent back to the spammer automatically. (It is

best to ueue your mail and send manually, rather than send

immediately, so that you can see what's about to go out before it's

actually sent. You should also turn off your mailer's automatic

honoring of return receipt requests, if any.) If you have a good

Internet service provider, you may

be able to forward copies of spam e-mail to the system administrators

who can route a complaint to the ISP of the spammer (or if you know a

lot about mail headers and DNS tools, you can probably contact these

ISPs yourself to complain about the spammer.) If you are getting

spammed a lot, there are a variety of filters and anti-spam

services available, including:

Spam Hater (http://www.cix.co.uk/~net-services/spam/spam_hater.htm) for Windows users;

TAG (
http://alcor.concordia.ca/topics/email/auto/procmail/spam)
for experienced Unix users;

SpamBouncer (http://www.spambouncer.org) for experienced
Unix users (works well with TAG);

BrightMail (http://www.brightmail.com/) for ISPs;

SpamCop (http://spamcop.net/) for anyone;

More information on fighting spam is available at:

Elsop's Anti-Spam Page (
http://www.elsop.com/wrc/nospam.htm);

MaximumDownforce's Info-n-Links Page(
http://www.maximumdownforce.com/hotlinks.html);

Whew's Anti-Spam Campaign (
http://www.whew.com/Spammers/).

Many of these are difficult to use for novices, and some require
Unix

expertise. Others are services that deal with ISPs only, not end
users.

Be conscious of Web security.

Never submit a credit card number or other highly sensitive

personal information without first making sure your connection
is

secure (encrypted). In Netscape, look for an closed lock
(Windows) or unbroken key (Mac) icon at the

bottom of the browser window. In Internet Explorer, look for a closed

lock icon at the bottom (Windows) or near the top (Mac) of the browser window.

In any browser, look at

the URL (Web address) line - a secure connection will begin "https://"

intead of "http://". If you are at page that asks for such information

but shows "http://" try adding the "s" yourself and hitting enter to

reload the page (for Netscape or IE; in another browser, use whatever method is re uired

by your browser to reload the page at the new URL). If you get an

error message that the page or site does not exist, this probably

means that the company is so clueless - and careless with your

information and your money - that they don't even have Web security.

Take your business elsewhere.

Your browser itself gives away information about you, if your IP address

can be tied to your identity (this is most commonly true of DSL and broadband users, rather than modem users, who are a dwindling minority.

Also be on the lookout for "spyware" - software that may be included

with applications you install (games, utilities, whatever), the

purpose of which is to silently spy on your online habits and other

details and report it back to the company whose product you are using.

One MS Windows solution for disabling spyware is the Ad-aware program

(shareware, from http://www.lavasoft.de/),

which can remove spyware from your computer; it is based on a large

collaboratively maintained database of information about spyware.

Linux and Mac products of this sort are likely to appear soon.

Java, Javascript and ActiveX can also be used for spyware purposes.

Support for these scripting languages can be disabled in your

browser's configuration options (a.k.a. preferences, settings,

or properties). It is safest to surf with them turned off,

and only turn them on when a site you trust and want to use

re□uires them.

Be conscious of home computer security.

On the other side of the coin, your own computer may be a trouble

spot for Internet security.

If you have a DSL line, broadband cable modem or other connection

to the Internet that is up and running 24 hours (including T1 at the office without a firewall

or NAT),

unlike a modem-and-phone-line connection, be sure to turn your computer off

when you are not using it. Most home PCs have pitifully poor security

compared to the Unix workstations that power most commercial Web

sites. System crackers search for vulnerable, unattended DSL-connected

home computers, and can invade them with surprising ease, rifiling

through files looking for credit card numbers or other sensitive data, or even "taking over" the computer and quietly using it for their own

purposes, such as lauching attacks on other computers elsewhere -

attacks you could initially be blamed for. Firewall hardware and software is

another option that can protect you from these kinds of attacks (available

at any computer store; freeware and shareware implementations may be

available at sites like http://www.shareware.com

or http://www.download.com.

Examine privacy policies and seals.

When you are considering whether or not to do business with a Web

site, there are other factors than a secure connection you have to consider that are equally

important to Web security. Does the site provide offline contact

information, including a postal address? Does the site have a

prominently-posted privacy policy? If so, what does it say? (Just

because they call it a "privacy policy" doesn't mean it will protect you - read it for yourself. Many are little more than disclaimers

saying that you have no privacy! So read them carefully.) If the

policy sounds OK to you, do you have a reason to believe it? Have you

ever heard of this company? What is their reputation? And are they

backing up their privacy statement with a seal program such as TRUSTe

http://www.truste.org/ or

BBBonline http://www.bbbonline.org/? (While imperfect, such

programs hold Web sites to at least some minimal baseline standards, and may revoke, with much fanfare, the

approval-seal licenses of bad-acting companies that do not

keep their word.) If you see a seal, is it real? Check with the

seal-issuing site to make sure the seal isn't a fake. And examine

terms carefully, especially if you are subscribing to a service rather

than buying a product. Look out for auto-rebilling scams and hidden

fees.

Remember that YOU decide what information about yourself to

reveal, when, why, and to whom.

Don't give out personally-identifiable information too easily. Just as

you might think twice about giving some clerk at the mall your home

address and phone number, keep in mind that simply because a site asks

for or demands personal information from you does not mean you have to

give it. You do have to give accurate billing information if you are

buying something, of course, but if you are registering with a free

site that is a little too nosy for you, there is no law (in most places) against

providing them with pseudonymous information. (However, it would

probably be polite to use obviously fake addresses, such as "123 No

Such Street, Nowhere, DC 01010". If they are generating mailings based on this information - presumably in accordance with the terms of their

privacy policy - they can probably weed such addresses out and not

waste the postage on them. Definitely do NOT use someone else's real

address!)

However, if you are required to agree to

terms of service before using the free service, be sure those terms

do not include a requirement that you provide correct information,

unless the penalty is simply not being allowed to use the service

any more, and you're willing to pay that price if they figure out

you are not providing them with your actual personally-identifiable

information.

Use encryption!

Last but certainly not least, there are other privacy threats

besides abusive marketers, nosy bosses, spammers and scammers. Some

of the threats include industrial espionage, government surveillance, identity theft, disgruntled former associates, and system crackers.

Relatively easy-to-use e-mail and file encryption software is

available for free, such as Pretty Good Privacy (PGP, available at: http://www.pgpi.org/), which runs on

almost all computers and even integrates seamlessly with most major

e-mail software. Good encryption uses very robust secret codes, that

are difficult if not impossible to crack, to protect your data. You

can also use specialized services (some free, some pay)

that go beyond infomediary services, including running all connections

through a securely encrypted "tunnel", anonymous dialup, even anonymous

Web publishing. Another type of product is SSH tunnelling (port forwarding) packages, such as FSecure SSH (http://www.fsecure.com/products/ssh/),

and SecureCRT (http://www.vandyke.com/products/securecrt/).

IF you want to learn how to survive in the wilderness

The Wilderness Survival Skills Everyone Should Know

 A few hours watching the Discovery Channel can prompt extreme survival fantasies involving frog licking and urine drinking, but what basic skills would you actually need to survive in the wilderness? Here's a look at the basics you need to become an adult Boy Scout straight from a cadre of survival experts.

Blast from the past is a weekly feature at Lifehacker in which we revive old, but still relevant, posts for your reading and hacking pleasure. This week, we're talking about how to rough it on your own, or survive out in the wilderness if you go camping, get caught away from your friends, or just need to make it home in one piece.

The key to surviving in the wilderness is preparation. But this post isn't about stockpiling food or preparing for disasters at home (although both are a good idea). This is about the skills and tricks you can learn and remember now that will help save your life if your car breaks down in the woods, you're lost while hiking, or a terrible disaster strands you in the wilderness. Before we get started on technique let's make a list of priorities to keep you alive and we'll go through them in more detail in a moment.

How to Prepare for and Survive a Disaster

I talked with survival teacher and founder of onPoint Tactical Kevin Reeve for help coming up with a list of priorities for survival in case of a disaster. This is what he suggests:

Immediate security: If the building is on fire, get out. If someone is shooting at you, move to cover. Whatever the immediate danger, get away from it.

First aid: Attend to any medical problems that may have happened in the original event. Check yourself for injuries and treat them.

Self protection: If you are at risk from predators, two-legged or four-legged, you must arm yourself. This might be a sharpened stick, a knife, machete, shotgun, or banjo. Just have something to attack the zombies with.

Physical needs (in order): Shelter, fire, water, food, and hygiene.

It's also worth noting that nearly every survivalist, doctor, paramedic, and teacher recommends one key survival tool everyone should follow: positivity. It seems silly, but it can provide you with the mental endurance to stay safe in any number of situations. A recent study in Psychological Science also suggests that your own perception of illness and the potential for treatment has an effect on the outcome. In short, the idea of mind over matter can help you survive.

Let's look at each of these in a little more detail, starting with your first priority after making sure you're not it in immediate danger: first aid.

Learn to Perform Basic First Aid Techni ues, Kit or No Kit

Basic first aid is a good life skill to have in general, but it's an essential survival skill to have in case of an emergency. Knowing how to fix three common injuries will usually get you by. Performing these on yourself will probably cause some tears, but at least you will be able to move to safety. I talked with firefighter and trained paramedic Philip Carlson to find the best solutions if you're stranded without a proper first aid kit.

Cut and Scrape First Aid

In most cases, you can ignore small cuts, but keep the wound clean and watch it for infection. If the injury is deep and you can't stop the blood your last resort is a tourniquet to stop the flow of blood. Tourniquets should be at least one-inch wide (a strip of shirt, belt, anything like that will work) and tightened around the limb above the injury. Tighten the tourniquet until the bright red bleeding stops and cover the injury with any clean material you have.

Mend Fractures and Dislocations

If you dislocate a bone you need to get in back in place. For shoulders, you can roll on the ground or hit it against a hard surface to reset the bone. Kneecaps can be popped back in place by stretching your leg out and forcing it into the socket. For fractures, you need to find material to create a splint. In the woods, a couple sticks will do the trick. Stabilize the fractured bone with the sticks and tie them together with shoelaces to hold the brace in place.

Treat Burns

To care for a first (reddening) or second degree (blistering) burn from fire, remove any clothing and find lukewarm water to run over the burn or coat it in honey if it's available. Wrap the burn loosely with a wet piece of clothing. If water is not available, clean out debris, dirt, and any loose skin as best you can and find water as soon as possible. Keep the wound elevated whenever possible and do not open any blisters that may have formed.

Self Protection

While Liam Neeson can get by punching wolves in the face, that's generally not the best way to approach a dangerous situation. Instead, it's best to get away from the animal slowly.

The Boy Scouts recommend a simple approach for wolves, coyotes, and cougars: face the animal and slowly back away from it. Don't play dead, run, or approach the animal. If you're cornered, make yourself as big as possible. Spread out your arms and make a lot of noise. If this still doesn't work, throw anything you can find at the animal.

If it comes down to it, you might have to weather an attack. In his book, Emergency, author Neil Strauss provides a means to defend against wild dogs that can apply to other animals in an emergency: If the animal does attack, block its mouth with your non-dominant arm and smash the heel of your hand into its snout or hit it in the eyes. If you can temporarily disable the animal, run and find a tree to hide in before you attempt first aid.

Physical Needs: Build a Shelter and Start a Fire

In order to survive, you need to maintain your body temperature. On one end of the spectrum, this means keeping warm, but you also need to know how to keep cool if you're caught in a desert. In either situation a shelter is your first order of business.

Build a Shelter to Protect You from the Elements

Even if you can start a fire with everything ranging from your glasses to a bottle of water, you're going to need a shelter at some point. Thankfully, the human body doesn't need the Hilton to survive, and your shelter only needs to meet two requirements: it has to block the elements and insulate for warmth.

Focus on finding a shelter that protects you from the ground, the wind, that insulates from the cold or heat, and protects you from rain and snow. A tarp or garbage bag is a lifesaver if stuffed with leaves or grass to form a wind/cold/rain barrier.

Once your shelter is built, it's time to make a fire.

How to Start a Fire with Nearly Anything

Firefighters recommend keeping two things in mind when starting a fire: the wind direction and the surrounding area. A fire is an important part of your survival, but you don't want to catch the entire forest on fire just to attract the attention of rescuers. The USDA Forest Service recommends building your campfire away from overhanging branches, rotten stumps, logs, dry grass, and leaves. Fire might have been one of the first things we humans learned how to make, but that doesn't mean it's easy to start a fire. Let's look at a few tricks for using materials you might already have.

Start a fire with eyeglasses: In order to properly start a fire with glasses, your best bet is a pair of far-sighted glasses, which better resemble a magnifying glass. To use eyeglasses, spit on the lens and use the lens to angle the sun at a pile of kindling (dry leaves, twigs, or Doritos all make great kindling). It will take a while, but your kindling will heat up enough and smolder. Carefully blow on the fire to start the flame.

Start a fire with a bottle of water: The same idea as the eye glasses can apply to a bottle of water (or a condom or ice). Focus the sun's rays through the water so that it creates a single point of heat. Eventually, it will catch fire.

Start a fire with you cell phone battery: The above two methods require a sunny day, but you won't always have that luxury. If you're stranded, there's a decent chance you have a lithium battery. It may be far-fetched, but if you also happen to have some steel wool you can create a short between the positive and negative terminals to cause a spark. If you don't have steel wool around, you can use your knife or any conductive material you can scavenge.

Start a fire with sticks: This is by far the hardest method, but it's also one of the most likely scenarios you might find yourself in. This method re□uires you to □uickly roll a stick on a log and use the friction to start a fire. This will take a while even if you have practice. The good news is that you can safely practice this in your own yard. It took me almost an hour to get a spark this way, but I leapt for joy when I did.

Physical Needs: Learn How to Find Water and Feed Yourself

Your fire-starting skills are great for keeping you warm, but you need to find something to eat and drink to keep you alive. Your first priority is water, so let's take a look at how you can find and sterilize water for drinking.

How to Find Water to Drink

In many parts of the country you can find water by following the sound of a flowing river, but that's not always the case. If you have trouble finding water, a few pieces of knowledge will help you on your way:

Grazing animals usually head to water near dawn and dusk. Following them can often lead you to water.

Flies and mos☐uitoes tend to stay within around 400 feet of water.

Dew that hangs on grass in a field is an excellent source of water. You can collect this by running an extra piece of cloth through the grass as you walk.

Stagnant water is not usually suitable to drink even if you can boil it.

In the desert you can often find water if you dig up a dry creek bed.

Once you find a source of water, bring it to a boil if possible. Even the cleanest of mountain streams can have microbes and parasites in the water. If boiling isn't not an option, search out water from a flowing stream or the dew on leaves. You can also create a filter by layering bark, stones, sand, and charcoal and running the water through the materials. Remember, no matter how hungry you are, water is more important to your survival. That said, you can settle your gurgling stomach as well. Let's look at how you can do it without killing yourself.

Learn the Big Four to Always Find Edible Plants

The easiest solution is to remember plants indigenous in most areas. Kevin Reeve suggests being familiar with four plants:

Acorn from Oak: The entire nut is edible and they're easy to stockpile.

Pine: The nuts and inner bark of the tree are edible. You can also make pine needle tea.

Cattail: This is one of best options out there. The base stalk is like celery, the root and tuber can make flour, and the pollen is very healthy.

Grass The corm (aka the base) is starchy, but edible and filled with water and carbohydrates.

Learn the Universal Edibility Test

You might have heard the old rule of thumb that you should follow animals around and eat what they eat, but that's not a foolproof method. In order to find if a plant is edible, you need to test it. You can follow the Universal Edibility Test, which re□uires you to place a small piece of plant against your lip, then your tongue, and finally in your whole mouth. Unfortunately, you have to wait for eight hours before you know if the plants safe to eat and it's still possible a plant can poison you.

If you're more of a berry fan, you can follow a simple mnemonic from former Green Barret Myke Hawke to remember which berries are edible:

White and yellow, kill a fellow. Purple and blue, good for you. Red... could be good, could be dead.

Like the edibility test, the mnemonic isn't fool proof, but it's useful if you have no other options.

Physical Needs: The Basic Hygiene You Can Ignore (and What Not To)

If you end up in a long-term survival situation you need to keep up with a few hygiene habits. For the most part, you can ignore a lot of it, but I spoke with Dr. Dan Weiswasser, a primary care physician in Massachusetts about a few hygienic issues you shouldn't ignore:

If you're keen to pay attention to hygiene while stranded somewhere, I would primarily address dental care. Dental pla□ue can build up in a hurry, and dental infections are painful, dangerous, and expensive to repair. Brushing and flossing re□uire relatively universal, rudimentary tools and can go a long way towards preventing such infections (you can make a toothbrush from birch or by just wiping your teeth with a clean piece of cloth).

Beyond that, I would say that a lot of hygiene consideration depends on what conditions are like where you are stranded. Bacteria and fungus flourish where it's moist, dark, and warm. If you're trapped in the jungle, you'll want to keep intertriginous areas (areas where skin touches skin such as the armpits, under breasts, in groin, between the toes, and in other skin folds) as dry and aired out as possible. Again, this can simply be an issue of wearing dry clothes. Baby powder or corn starch can also be helpful for absorbing moisture.

But what do you do when the call of nature is too strong and you need to find toilet paper? Kevin Reeve has a simple solution:

As for primitive toilet paper, in the winter, a snowball is actually □uite invigorating, but most of the time, leaves of a plant like mullein are the go-to method. Sometimes an unopened pine cone will work, but ouch! One of the keys to this is to s□uat not sit. This forces the cheeks apart and means that there will be far less cleaning necessary.

Navigation Methods to Help You Find Your Way Home

If you're lost, the Boy Scouts recommend a simple mnemonic: STOP (Stop, Think, Observe, Plan). In most cases, you want to stay where you are and wait for help to come. If it starts to get late, you can build your shelter, start your fire and search for food. If help doesn't come, it's time to move on. The first thing you need to do is find north.

In order to figure out your basic directions, remember that the sun sets in the west and rises in the east (just think about which coast starts their work day earlier if you struggle to remember this). There's also a few simple tricks that will help you find north quickly,

Use your watch to find north.

Locate the Big Dipper in the night sky to find the North Star.

Finding north is only half the battle. You still need to know which direction to head. If you have a general understanding of an area, head toward the nearest road or town. If you don't know the area, follow a water source downstream, or head toward a clearing where you can better signal for help.

How to Get Rescued

In order to get rescued, you need to know the most basic hand signals to alert a helicopter or plane you see pass overhead. Curiously, a wave is considered a sign to not land. Instead, if you see a helicopter or plane, form your arms in a "Y" as if you're ready to perform the Village People's "YMCA".

If you have a signalling tool like a flare, flashlight, or mirror, make use of them the second you see a rescue helicopter. Reflect the sun off the mirror in the direction of the helicopter to attract its attention.

If you hear rescuers in the distance but don't have any way to signal them, you can call in a deep voice. Normal natural sounds are usually a high pitch. Call out in a low tone so rescuers know you're a human.

No one expects to be caught in a potentially dangerous and extreme situation such as a natural disaster. If the unthinkable does occur, having a plan and knowing what to do could make all the difference for you and your loved ones.

These 3 general tips can help you stay safe during a disaster.

1. If you have not been ordered to evacuate, stay in a safe area or shelter during a natural disaster. In your home, a safe area may be a ground floor interior room, closet or bathroom. Be sure you have access to your survival kit in case you are in an emergency event that lasts several days.

2. Listen to your portable radio for important updates and instructions from local authorities. Remember to have a battery-powered radio in your survival kit. Some radios are now equipped with multiple power sources, such as batteries, solar panels and a hand crank.

3. If power is lost, use a generator with caution. Make sure conditions are safe before operating a portable generator. Only operate it outside — away from windows, doors or vents. Follow all manufacturer's instructions.

4. Stay in your safe area and do not drive until the danger has passed. Resist the temptation to check on your property until you are sure it is safe to do s

If there are only moments to spare, you need to know how to react to everything from an earthquake to a tornado and a flood to hurricane

A natural disaster is a devastating event caused by rain, wind, fire, and even earth that endangers people's lives and property. Although there is often little that can be done to prevent a natural disaster, people can take steps to reduce the effect that it has on themselves and their property. When it comes to our homes, it is important to know how to prepare for the numerous threats from nature. Not only will this save your property from excessive damage, but it may also help to save the lives of loved ones.

Conclusion

"in the field of observation, chance favors the prepared mind" (Quotery.com). Food storage is a good place to start, but preparedness extends to just about every part of a person's life. Practices such as budgeting your money, carrying out necessary home and car repairs, and obtaining every kind of insurance, are all ways in which we protect ourselves against an unknown future. Keep an emergency survival kit in your home and car, and include important and potentially life-saving items inside. If you take these sorts of things seriously, when the worst does happen, the situation itself will be far less serious. Preparedness is not something that is reserved for those who are fanatic or obsessive; it is something that is important for anyone who cares about protecting their life, and the lives of those close to them in the face of a future that will forever remain a mystery.

Even if a disaster is not immediately threatening your family, it's a good idea to keep an emergency kit in your home, and make sure the entire family knows exactly where it's located. That way, if there's any type of emergency or disaster, your family will know where there are supplies to help. For each natural disaster scenario, consider sitting down with your family and making a plan.

It's human nature to avoid thinking about these worst-case scenarios. After all, none of us want to imagine a pandemic sweeping the country, or a tornado barreling through our own neighborhood. But these things do happen, and the best thing we can do is to prepare for these events. Even a little bit of preparedness can make a big difference.

About The Author

My name is MARY DAVENPORT, I am the founder and owner of THE ACT OF CREATIVITY (TAOC).

I am first and foremost a mother of 3, grandmother of 8. Have been freelancing for many years now , as a writer before I setup my own organization, i am also currently an hotel general manager and an avid reader..my favorite is kindle publishing though..lol I really love educating people on how to become successful in life, stay healthy and live the life of their dreams

Do not go yet; One last thing to do

If you enjoyed this book or found it useful I'd be very grateful if you'd post a short review on it. Your support really does make a difference and I read all the reviews personally so I can get your feedback and make this book even better.

Thanks again for your support!